MICRO WAYS TO A MAN'S HEART

Compiled by The Helpful '8'

Edited by
GILLIAN BURR

Illustrated by Jane Finestone

VALLENTINE MITCHELL

First published 1985 in Great Britain by
VALLENTINE MITCHELL AND COMPANY LIMITED
Gainsborough House, 11 Gainsborough Road,
London E11 1RS, England

and in the United States of America by
VALLENTINE MITCHELL AND COMPANY LIMITED
c/o Biblio Distribution Centre
81 Adams Drive, P.O. Box 327, Totowa, N.J. 07511

ISBN 0 85303 218 1

*Cover photograph: china and cutlery
by courtesy of Chinacraft Ltd*

Printed in Great Britain by
Robert Hartnoll Ltd, Bodmin

Dear Cooks,

Due to the success of our first three cookbooks in the series "Way To A Man's Heart" we have ventured to keep up with the times and have now produced a microwave cookbook, *Micro Ways To A Man's Heart.* All proceeds from the book will go to the Central British Fund for World Jewish Relief. Microwave ovens are a wonderful aid to a busy cook. Dishes that may in the past have taken two to three hours to cook are now cooked to perfection in around 45 minutes. Another great advantage of cooking in a microwave oven is less washing up – marvellous for good family relationships!

Many people have again given their time to help produce this book and our most grateful thanks go to the following: to Ann Harris for Kashrut advice, and to Lesley Bennett, Bettina Bradfield, Rosanna Burr, Carole Chesterman, Jennifer Davis, Gillian Fenner, Pat Fine, Jane Finestone, Rosemary Fisch, Barbara Green, Valerie Greenbury, Miki Hildebrand, Deanna Kaye, Renata Knobil, Helen Meller, Anne Moss, Ruth Starr, Beverly Stoplar, Marilyn Unger and Bondi Zimmerman.

The Helpful '8' Committee

Many men live without love –
What is passion but pining?
But where is the man who can live without dining?
We may live without friends, we may live without books,
But civilized men cannot live without cooks.

From "Lucille" by Owen Meredith

CONTENTS

MEASURES AND OVEN TEMPERATURE GUIDE

Whilst every effort has been made to ensure that the recipes conform to Jewish dietary laws, we have had to leave it to you, the cook, to check on the Kashrut of some individual ingredients, e.g. wine, cheese, wine vinegar, gelatine, etc.

DRY MEASURE

	1 oz	28 grms
	2 oz	56 grms
	3 oz	85 grms
	3½oz	100 grms
(¼ lb)	4 oz	114 grms
	5 oz	142 grms
	6 oz	170 grms
	7 oz	198 grms
(½ lb)	8 oz	225 grms
(¼ kilo)	8¾oz	250 grms
	9 oz	256 grms
	10 oz	283 grms
	11 oz	312 grms
	12 oz	340 grms
	13 oz	368 grms
	14 oz	400 grms
	15 oz	425 grms
(1 lb)	16 oz	450 grms
(½ kilo)	17½oz	500 grms
	1½lbs	700 grms

LIQUID MEASURE

1 tablespoon	1 tablespoon
2 tablespoons	2 tablespoons (1½ DL)
3 tablespoons	3 tablespoons
4 tablespoons	4 tablespoons
5 tablespoons	1 decilitre
6 tablespoons	1¼ decilitres
8 tablespoons (¼ pint)	1½ decilitres
¼ pint – generous	2 decilitres
½ pint – scant	¼ litre (2½ DL)
½ pint	3 decilitres
¾ pint	½ litre – scant
¾ pint – generous	½ litre
1 pint	½ litre – generous
1¼ pints	¾ litre
1½ pints	1 litre – scant
1¾ pints	1 litre
2 pints	1 litre – generous
2½ pints	1¼ litres
3 pints	1½ litres
3½ pints	2 litres
4 pints	2¼ litres
4¼ pints	2½ litres
5 pints	3 litres

OVEN TEMPERATURE GUIDE

Gas No.	Fahrenheit	Centigrade	Description
¼	225	120	
½	250	140	Very Cool
1	275	150	
2	300	160	Cool or Slow
3	325	180	
4	350	185	Moderate
5	375	190	
6	400	200	Moderately Hot
7	425	220	
8	450	230	Hot
9	475	240	Very Hot

2 level tablespoons of flour = 1 oz
A British pint = 20 fl ozs
A British cup = 10 fl ozs

1 level tablespoon of sugar = 1 oz
An American pint = 16 fl ozs
An American cup = 8 fl ozs

MICROWAVE "KNOW-HOW"

Getting to know how your microwave oven works will make your use of it far more rewarding. This book is intended to be a cookbook not a handbook. Most manufacturers provide a manual with their ovens and I would recommend reading yours very carefully.

Advantages of cooking in a microwave oven.

Cooking in a microwave oven is far cheaper than cooking in a conventional oven.

Far quicker.

Less washing up and no dirty oven to clean.

No need to move food from saucepans to serving dishes; the food may be served in the dish in which it is cooked provided it has no metal decoration. Vegetables cooked in a microwave oven keep more of their vitamins, do not lose their bright colour and have a better flavour than when cooked by any other method.

Sauces are less likely to curdle or stick when cooked in the oven and do not require constant stirring.

Making the most of your oven

Dinner party. Vegetables may be cooked in the morning separately, and then a selection may be arranged attractively on a platter and reheated just before serving – very useful when entertaining guests.

Someone coming home late. When the rest of the family are being served, the food for the latecomer may be plated, covered with pricked cling film and then just re-heated for 2½ minutes on their return. The food will have retained its freshness.

Unexpected guests. Provided you have some food in your freezer, or there is a super-market nearby, chops, chicken portions, mince meat, fish and pasta dishes may be defrosted in a microwave oven in a matter of minutes and then may be cooked or reheated in the microwave oven again within minutes.

Forgotten to take the butter out of the freezer or fridge in time? Place the butter in the oven on full power for a few seconds.

Melted chocolate required. No longer do you have to melt chocolate in a bowl over a pan of hot water, stirring frequently. Just place the chocolate in a bowl in the oven and heat on medium power for 2–3 minutes, stirring just once after 1½ minutes.

DO'S AND DON'TS

DO   find out the power of your machine – the recipes in this book are based on a 650 watt machine, so if yours has a lower power the dishes may take a little longer to cook, if your machine is more powerful the cooking times may be shorter.

DO   turn your cooking dish during the course of cooking once or twice if your oven does not have turntable. This will ensure that the food is cooked evenly all over.

DO   experiment with your own recipes. You will often find that dishes require less sugar and salt, as the natural flavour of the food is much stronger when cooked in a microwave oven.

DO   see that any food that is being cooked together is made up of similar sized pieces so that they cook at the same rate i.e. potatoes, meat etc.

DO   use a larger cooking container than usual as food expands considerably in a microwave oven.

DON'T	use metal dishes in the oven or anything decorated with gold or silver.
DON'T	use any lead crystal glass in a microwave oven.
DON'T	cook pastry or bread or breadcrumbed dishes covered, just rest a little kitchen paper on them to absorb any excess moisture.
DON'T	cook eggs in their shells, they will burst.

SOME OF YOUR QUESTIONS ANSWERED

Q   What is a microwave?

A microwave is a short wave rather like a radio wave but shorter. A microwave is reflected by metal:

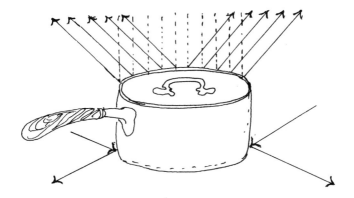

A microwave is transmitted or passes through china, glass, paper and Pyrex without heating it:

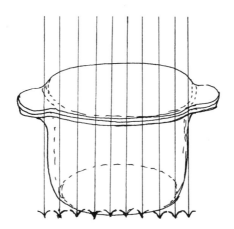

9

A microwave is absorbed by water molecules:

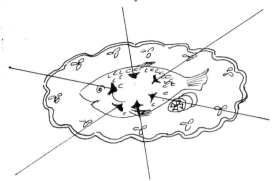

The microwaves produce heat by friction caused by moisture molecules in the food vibrating against each other very quickly. This is the same friction heat you experience when you rub your hands together on a cold day to warm them.

The microwaves penetrate into the food at the rate of 2450 million per second and for 1½" into the food from the outside in.

If the food is thicker than 3", the centre will cook by conduction of heat rather than by direct microwave action:

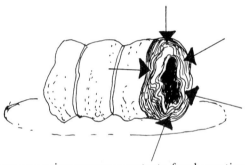

To sum up: microwaves penetrate food creating quick heat, but they will not directly heat the oven cavity or the container the food is in. This makes for economic, fast cooking.

Q What would happen if I put a metal container in the microwave oven?
A The metal would cause arcing (sparking) which can seriously damage the electronic components. Turn the machine off immediately and remove the dish.
Q Why do some foods pop in a microwave oven?
A They are being cooked too quickly, try to cook on a lower power.
Q How do I clean my oven?
A Wipe out after use with a damp cloth or a soapy one, but should a stubborn mark appear, place a jug of water in the oven and heat until it boils for 2–3 minutes. The resulting steam should loosen the stain and a damp cloth should then remove it.

STARTERS

ARTICHOKE APPETISER   Gillian Burr

Serves 4–6   **Preparation 10 minutes**   **Cook 11 minutes**

1 oz butter (28 grms)

1 small onion finely chopped

1 clove garlic crushed

14 oz tin artichoke hearts drained and chopped (395 grms)

4 eggs beaten

1 oz fresh breadcrumbs (28 grms)

½ teaspoon oregano

A few drops Tabasco sauce

8 oz strong Cheddar cheese grated (225 grms)

1 tbl parsley chopped

This recipe is cooked throughout on full power. Melt butter for 1 minute, add onion and garlic and cook for 3 minutes. Add the artichokes, breadcrumbs, oregano, Tabasco, cheese, parsley, egg and salt to taste, and mix well. Spread evenly in a large shallow dish. Cook for 7 minutes. Allow to stand for 4 minutes then cut it into portions and serve. This dish may be cut into cubes and served with drinks.

ARTICHOKE AND SPINACH MOUNDS

Preparation 5 minutes

	2 servings	4 servings	6 servings
Frozen or tinned artichoke bottoms	7 oz (198 grms)	14 oz (395 grms)	1½ lbs (675 grms)
Spinach frozen	6 oz (170 grms)	12 oz (335 grms)	1 lb (450 grms)
Onion	1 small	1 medium	1 large
Butter/Margarine	1 oz (28 grms)	2 oz (56 grms)	3 oz (85 grms)
Nutmeg	shake	a pinch	¼ teaspoon

Salt and black pepper to taste

Hollandaise sauce (see Sauce section)

Place frozen artichoke bottoms in shallow dish, cover with pricked cling film and cook on full power for 5 (6) (7) minutes until tender. Reserve. If using tinned artichoke bottoms place in a shallow dish with 1 (2) (3) tablespoons of water and cook on full power until hot.

Place butter in a shallow dish and melt on full power for 30 (40) (50) seconds, add onion and cook for another minute, add the spinach, nutmeg, salt and pepper and stir. Cook covered with pricked cling film for 5 (6) (7) minutes, check seasoning. With a spoon carefully place spinach mounds on the hot artichoke bottoms. Reheat when required. Delicious as a starter served with Hollandaise sauce.

BROCCOLI SOUFFLE
Dorice Smith

Serves 4　　　　　**Preparation 5 minutes**　　　　　**Cook 12 minutes**

20 oz frozen broccoli cooked and chopped　　4 eggs
　(560 grms)**or**　　　　　　　　　　　　　　**12 fl oz milk** (341 ml)
2 lbs fresh broccoli cooked and chopped　　**4 oz butter** (113 grms)
　(900 grms)　　　　　　　　　　　　　　**12 oz seasoned breadcrumbs** (341 grms)

Melt butter on full power for 30 seconds. Beat eggs and add milk and butter, then mix in the breadcrumbs and broccoli. Place in greased casserole and cook on full power for 10–12 minutes.

POOR MAN'S CAVIAR
Bernice Burr

Serves 6　　　**Preparation 5 minutes**　　　**Cook 6 minutes**　　　**Chill 1 hour**

2 large aubergines　　　　　　　　　2 tbls lemon juice
1 large onion chopped　　　　　　　**Salt, pepper and paprika to taste**
4 tbls oil　　　　　　　　　　　　　*Garnish:* **Parsley sprigs and black olives**

Remove flesh from aubergines and cut into small pieces, sauté them with the onion in the oil on full power until they are very soft, 5 minutes approximately. Add rest of ingredients and either purée or mash. Place in shallow dish, cover and chill for at least 1 hour. Garnish and serve with toast.

CORN ON THE COB
Mrs Corny

Preparation 2 minutes

	1 serving	*2 servings*	*4 servings*
Corn, fresh or frozen	1	2	4
Butter	½ **oz** (14 grms)	1 **oz** (28 grms)	2 **oz** (56 grms)
Freshly ground black pepper			
Salt			

Melt butter in a casserole dish on full power. Place the corn in the dish, wrap greaseproof paper loosely round them and cook on full power for 5 (9) (12) minutes. Sprinkle with salt and black pepper. Delicious!

EGGS FLORENTINE

Serves 4   **Preparation 2 minutes**   **Cook 9 minutes**

8 oz frozen chopped spinach (225 grms)   4 eggs
1 oz butter (28 grms)   Salt and pepper to taste
A pinch nutmeg   4 ramekin dishes

Place spinach in a bowl, cover with pricked cling film and cook on full power for 6–8 minutes stirring occasionally. Beat in the butter, nutmeg and seasonings and divide the mixture between the dishes. Break an egg into each dish and prick the yolks with a pin, season and cover each dish with pricked cling film. Cook on full power for 2½ minutes and then allow to stand for 2 minutes before serving.

HOT GRAPEFRUIT STARTER

Preparation 5 minutes

	2 servings	*4 servings*	*6 servings*
Large grapefruit	1	2	3
Brown sugar	2 teaspoons	1 tbl	1½ tbls
Sherry	2 tbls	4 tbls	6 tbls
Butter/Margarine	1 teaspoon	2 teaspoons	3 teaspoons

Cut grapefruit in half and carefully separate each segment removing any pips. Sprinkle the cut surface with sugar and sherry and dot with butter. Cook on full power for 6 (7) (8) minutes until hot.

HADDOCK MOUSSE   Sally Friend

Serves 4   **Preparation 20 minutes**   **Cook 7 minutes**   **Chill 3 hours**

1 lb haddock fillets (450 grms)   2 egg whites
2 tbls white wine vinegar   8 fl oz hot water (227 ml)
1 level tbl kosher powdered gelatine   Salt and pepper to taste
3 eggs hardboiled   *Sauce*
¼ pint mayonnaise (142 ml)   ½ pint mayonnaise (284 ml)
1 tbl tomato purée   1 bunch watercress trimmed and washed
1 teaspoon anchovy essence   *Garnish:* **1 sprig of dill**

Arrange fish in a single layer in a shallow dish. Cover with pricked cling film and cook on full power for 6 minutes or until tender. Flake the fish. Discard any bones and skin. Melt the gelatine in the vinegar and hot water as the gelatine packet instructions. Place all the other ingredients except the egg whites in a food processor and mix, gradually stir in the gelatine. Tip into a bowl and place in a refrigerator until the mixture is thick enough to coat the back of a spoon. Whisk the egg whites until stiff and fold into the fish mixture. Pour the mixture into a ring mould and refrigerate until set – 3 hours.

Sauce: Finely chop the watercress, and mix it with the mayonnaise. Turn out the mousse onto a serving dish. Spoon over a little of the sauce and garnish with a sprig of dill. Serve the remaining mayonnaise separately. Delicious as a starter or a special luncheon dish.

IMAM BAILDI   Bernice Burr

Serves 6   **Preparation 10 minutes**   **Cook 10 minutes**

3 aubergines
Filling
4 onions chopped
2 tbls olive oil
1 teaspoon brown sugar

3 heaped tbls tomato purée
½ cup fresh breadcrumbs
2 tbls pine nuts
12 black olives
Salt and black pepper to taste

Cut the aubergines in half and cover them with pricked cling film and cook on full power for 3 minutes to soften them. Remove the pulp leaving about ¼ inch (½ cm) of flesh round the shells. Chop the pulp and reserve.

Filling: Fry the onions in the oil and add the chopped aubergine pulp and the remainder of the filling ingredients and mix well with just enough water to moisten. Place the filling in the shells, decorate with the black olives, add a little oil and cook for 7 minutes approximately.

LEEKS A LA GRECQUE   Jennifer Davis

Preparation 5 minutes   **Cook 18–20 minutes**   **Chill 3 hours minimum**   **Advance**

	2 servings	*4 servings*	*6 servings*
Small white leeks	4	8	16
Small red pepper in fine strips	½	1 small	1 large
Court bouillon			
Tomatoes peeled and chopped	2	4	6
Olive oil	2 tbls	4 tbls	6 tbls
Water	2½ fl oz (70 ml)	¼ pint (142 ml)	6 fl oz (170 ml)
Salt	¼ teaspoon	½ teaspoon	¾ teaspoon
Black peppercorns	6	12	18
Coriander seeds	6	12	18
Bay leaf	½	1	1½
Parsley sprigs	3	6	9
Celery stick with leaves	½	1 small	1 medium
Clove garlic crushed	1 small	1 medium	2 small
Dry white wine	2½ fl oz (70 ml)	¼ pint (142 ml)	7 fl oz (200 ml)

Court bouillon: Place oil, wine, water, salt, pepper, coriander, bay leaf, garlic, parsley and celery in a large bowl and cook in a microwave oven on full power until they come to the boil, 2 minutes approximately, then cook on low power for another 2 minutes. Add leeks and tomato flesh, cover with pricked cling film and cook on low power until leeks are tender, 6 (8) (11) minutes approximately. Carefully remove leeks onto serving dish. Add the strips of red pepper to court bouillon and cook until tender 2–3 minutes. Remove the strips of red pepper and arrange them on top of the leeks. Cook the court bouillon on full power until reduced to 1 fl oz (28 ml), 2½ fl oz (72 ml), 3½ fl oz (100 ml) approximately. Correct seasoning and strain over leeks. Place in a refrigerator.

CHOPPED LIVER
Diane Taylor

Serves 6   **Preparation 15 minutes**   **Cook 19 minutes**   **Advance**

1 lb chicken livers (450 grms)
5 eggs hardboiled
½ lb Tomor (225 grms)

1 large Spanish onion finely sliced
1 Telma chicken cube
Salt and pepper to taste

Garnish: **1 hard boiled egg chopped, optional**

Place 2 oz (56 grms) Tomor in a bowl and cook on full power for 1 minute until melted, add finely sliced onion and cook on full power for 3 minutes until it is very soft. Add the liver cut into very small pieces and cook on full power for 2 minutes. Cover with pricked cling film and cook on half power for 12 minutes. When the liver is cooked, mix with the rest of the margarine and five eggs and process in a Magimix or mincer until required consistency. Garnish with the hard boiled egg.

CHOPPED LIVER
Sheilagh Goodman

Serves 4   **Cook 9½–10½ minutes**   **Advance**

8 oz chicken livers (225 grms)
1½ oz chicken fat (42 grms)
2 medium onions finely chopped
2 hard boiled eggs

Salt and pepper to taste
3 pint glass bowl (1.70 litres)
Garnish
Parsley sprigs
A few lettuce leaves

This recipe is cooked on full power throughout. Place the fat in the bowl and heat on full power for 1½ minutes, add the onions and coat them in the fat and cook for 4 minutes. Stir in the livers and heat for another 4–5 minutes (until the livers are just cooked) stirring them once half way through the cooking time. Allow them to stand for 5 minutes. Place the eggs in a food processor and process them for a few seconds, then place them in a small bowl. Next process the onions and livers and remaining fat for 5–6 seconds. Mix with most of the reserved eggs and place on bed of lettuce. Decorate top with the remaining egg and sprigs of parsley.

An alternative is to add ½ teaspoon tarragon or basil to the livers when cooking them.

MICROWAVE MUSHROOMS — Bettina Bradfield

Preparation 10 minutes   **Cook 3½–4½ minutes**   **Cool 3 hours**   **Advance**

	2 servings	*4 servings*	*6 servings*
Mushrooms sliced	**8 oz** (225 grms)	**12 oz** (340 grms)	**1 lb** (450 grms)
Basil leaves chopped	**5**	**10**	**14**
Small sticks fresh thyme chopped	**4**	**8**	**12**
Clove garlic chopped	**1 small**	**1 medium**	**1 large**
Oregano chopped	**½ teaspoon**	**1 teaspoon**	**1½ teaspoons**
Butter	**¾ oz** (21 grms)	**1½ oz** (42 grms)	**2¼ oz** (63 grms)
Sherry	**½ tbl**	**1 tbl**	**1½ tbls**
Lime juice	**½ lime**	**1 lime**	**1½ limes**

This recipe is cooked on full power throughout. Melt butter in bowl for 1 minute, add the herbs and mushrooms, sherry and lime juice stirring well. Cook for 3½ (4) (4½) minutes. Serve cold with hot toast or French bread.

NOODLES IN WALNUT SAUCE

Serves 2 as a main course and 4 as a starter   Preparation 5 mins.   Cook 15 mins.

3 oz butter softened (85 grms)
2 tbls plain flour
½ pint milk (284 ml)
4 oz walnut pieces chopped (113 grms)

1 clove garlic crushed
10 oz green tagliatelle freshly cooked (280 grms)
4 oz cheese grated (113 grms)

Place 1 oz (28 grms) of butter with the garlic in a bowl and cook on full power for 30 seconds until butter has melted. Stir in flour and gradually add the milk. Cook on full power until it comes to the boil stirring every minute. Cook on low power for 4 minutes, season to taste. Add rest of butter, 2 oz (56 grms), to the tagliatelle whilst it is still hot and sprinkle over the walnut pieces. Either leave the tagliatelle in one bowl or divide it between four individual dishes. Cover the tagliatelle with the white sauce and sprinkle with the cheese. Cook on full power until the cheese has melted or place under a hot grill until the cheese bubbles and turns brown.

STUFFED TOMATOES

Lynne Goldwyn

Preparation 10 minutes

Advance

	2 servings	*4 servings*	*6 servings*
Tomatoes very large	2	4	6
Butter	½ oz (14 grms)	1 oz (28 grms)	1½ oz (42 grms)
Medium sized mushrooms chopped	2	4	6
Fresh white breadcrumbs	1 tbl	2 tbls	3 tbls
Parmesan cheese	½ tbl	1 tbl	1½ tbls
Onion chopped	1 small	1 medium	1 large
Clove garlic crushed	1 small	1 medium	1 large
Salt and black pepper to taste			
Freshly fried bread cut into 2 inch rounds (5 cms)			

This recipe is cooked on full power throughout. Cut tops off tomatoes and reserve. Cut a thin slice from the bottom of the tomatoes so they stand firmly on their bases. Remove the pulp from the tomatoes with a teaspoon, discarding the cores. Place the butter in a shallow dish and cook for 30–40 seconds until melted, stir in the onion and garlic and cook for 1 (1½) (2) minutes. Add the mushrooms and mix well then cook for another 1–2 minutes. Stir in the tomato flesh and breadcrumbs and season to taste. Spoon the mixture into the tomato shells. Replace the lids and place them in a ring shape on a plate or in a shallow dish. Sprinkle the tomatoes with the cheese. The dish at this point could be placed in a refrigerator until required, and then cooked. Finish the dish by cooking the tomatoes for 4 (5) (6) minutes. Place each tomato on a round of fried bread and serve hot.

SOUPS

CREAM OF ARTICHOKE SOUP
Gillian Burr

Preparation 20 minutes   Advance   Freezable

	2 servings	*4 servings*	*6 servings*
Jerusalem artichokes			
peeled and sliced	½ **lb** (225 grms)	1 **lb** (450 grms)	1½ **lbs** (675 grms)
Butter	1 **oz** (28 grms)	1½ **oz** (42 grms)	2 **oz** (56 grms)
Egg	1 small	1 medium	1 large
Onion chopped	1 small	1 medium	1 large
Flour	½ **oz** (14 grms)	¾ **oz** (21 grms)	1¼ **oz** (35 grms)
Water boiling	½ **pint** (284 ml)	¾ **pint** (425 ml)	1¼ **pints** (710 ml)
Milk	½ **pint + 2 fl oz** (284ml + 60 ml)	¾ **pint + 2 fl oz** (425 ml + 60 ml)	1 **pint + 2 fl oz** (710 ml + 60 ml)
Single cream	1¼ **fl oz** (35 ml)	1¾ **fl oz** (50 ml)	2½ **fl oz** (74 ml)

Place onions in a large bowl with the butter and cook on full power for 45 seconds. Add artichokes and turn them in the butter. Cook on full power for 4 minutes stirring once during that time. Add the water and seasoning. Cover with pricked cling film and cook on ¾ power for 8 (10) (13) minutes. Purée the soup and sieve it. Cream the 2 fl oz (60 ml) of milk into the flour and gradually stir into the soup. Bring to the boil on full power stirring every minute. Add the rest of the milk and stir once and simmer on ½ power for 2 minutes. Mix the cream with the egg and stir into the soup. Heat again, still covered, on simmer power for another minute stirring once or twice. Do not allow to boil.

CREAM OF ARTICHOKE SOUP
Judy Jackson

Preparation 15–20 minutes   Advance   Freezable

	2 servings	*4 servings*	*6 servings*
Butter	1 tbl	2 tbls	3 tbls
Button mushrooms sliced	2 **oz** (56 grms)	¼ **lb** (113 grms)	6 **oz** (170 grms)
Onion chopped medium	1	2	3
Jerusalem artichokes			
peeled and sliced	½ **lb** (225 grms)	1 **lb** (450 grms)	1½ **lbs** (675 grms)
Vegetable stock	¼ **pint** (140 ml)	½ **pint** (¼ litre)	¾ **pint** (½ litre)
Milk	¼ **pint** (140 ml)	½ **pint** (¼ litre)	¾ **pint** (½ litre)
Salt and pepper to taste			

Melt half the butter in a large bowl on medium power. Stir in the sliced mushrooms and cook on full power for 20 (30) (40) seconds, stir again and cook for a few more seconds until mushrooms are lightly cooked. Transfer with their juice to another bowl. Melt the remaining butter and cook the onions and artichokes in the same way stirring them three times until they are soft. Add the mushrooms and juice with the vegetable stock and season well. Stir again. Cover the dish with pricked cling film and cook on full power for 2–3 minutes. Purée the vegetables and stock until smooth. Stir in the milk. Reheat when required.

BEETROOT AND CELERY SOUP

Preparation 10 minutes   Advance

	2 servings	4 servings	6 servings
Onion finely chopped	1 small	1 medium	1 large
Butter or margarine	1 teaspoon	2 teaspoons	1 dessertspoon
Plain flour	1 teaspoon	2 teaspoons	1 dessertspoon
Boiling water	½ pint (284 ml)	1 pint (570 ml)	1½ pints (850 ml)
Red wine	2 tbls	2½ tbls	3 tbls
Parve/chicken stock cube	1	2	3
Top of the milk	2 tbls	3 tbls	4 tbls
Mustard powder	1 pinch	½ teaspoon	¾ teaspoon
Powdered bay leaves	1 pinch	½ teaspoon	¾ teaspoon
Cooked beetroot	4 oz (113 grms)	6 oz (170 grms)	8 oz (225 grms)
Celery chopped	½ stick	1 stick	1½ sticks
Chives chopped	¾ tbl	1¼ tbls	1½ tbls
Sour cream (optional)	2 tbls	3 tbls	4 tbls

Salt and freshly ground black pepper to taste

Place onion, celery and butter in a bowl and place in microwave oven on full power for 3 minutes, stirring once during that time. Mix in the flour, stir the stock cube into the hot water and gradually add it to the flour stirring all the time. Stir in the wine. Add the mustard powder, bay leaves, beetroot, salt and pepper. Microwave on full power for 10 (14) (17) minutes. Purée the soup and then return to bowl and reheat on high for approximately 1–2 minutes until really hot. Garnish with chives and sour cream if desired. This soup is also delicious served chilled.

CARROT, CHEESE AND CAULIFLOWER SOUP Zena Clayton

Serves 8   Preparation 10 minutes   Cook 12 minutes   Advance   Freezable

1 small cauliflower finely chopped
6 oz carrots sliced thinly (170 grms)
1 medium onion thinly sliced
1½ pints hot parve chicken stock
  (scant litre)
Black pepper to taste

1 bay leaf
1 clove garlic crushed
2 oz curd/cottage cheese
  (56 grms)
2 tbls chopped parsley
A pinch sea salt

Place carrots, onions and cauliflower in a large bowl with the stock and add the pepper, salt and bay leaf, cook on full power until it comes to the boil, then simmer on medium power for 9 minutes, stirring once or twice. Remove the bay leaf and purée the rest of the ingredients with the cheese and garlic. Return to the bowl and stir in the parsley. Serve hot.

CARROT AND ORANGE SOUP — Bondia Zimmerman

Preparation 10 minutes   **Advance**   **Freezable**

	2 servings	4 servings	6 servings
Carrots medium size sliced	2	3	4
Cold water	2 fl oz (3 tbls)	3 fl oz (4 tlbs)	¼ pint (114 ml)
Onions chopped	1 small	1 medium	1 large
Celery sticks sliced	1 small	1 medium	1 large
Sugar granulated	½ teaspoon	¾ teaspoon	1 teaspoon
Oil	1 tbl	1½ tbls	2 tbls
Orange juice unsweetened	3 fl oz (4 tbls)	4½ fl oz (130 ml)	8 fl oz (227 ml)
Parve chicken stock cubes	1	1½	2
Boiling water	¾ pt (½ litre)	1⅓ pints (¾ litre)	2 pints (1¼ litres)
Cloves whole	1	1½	2
Lemon juice	a squeeze	½ teaspoon	1 teaspoon
Coriander	a pinch	½ teaspoon	1 teaspoon
Double cream	3 fl oz (90 ml)	6 fl oz (170 ml)	½ pint (280 ml)

Salt and cayenne pepper to taste

Garnish
Orange rind in thin shreds, blanched

Place carrots, onion, celery, sugar and oil with the cold water in a large bowl and cover with pricked cling film. Cook on full power for 8 (9) (10) minutes. Stir once during cooking and allow to stand for 2 minutes. Transfer the soup to a blender and add half the boiling water with the crumbled cubes and orange juice. When puréed, return the mixture to the large bowl. Stir in the remaining boiling water, coriander, cloves, lemon juice and cream. Season to taste. Cover with pricked cling film and cook for 3 (3½) (4) minutes on medium power. Stir and leave to stand for 2 minutes. Remove cloves. Stir once more and garnish with some blanched thin strips of orange rind.

CLEAR CHICKEN SOUP

Preparation 15 minutes   **Standing time 4 hours**   **Advance**   **Freezable**

	4 servings	6 servings	8 servings
Fowl cleaned	1½ lbs (675 grms)	2 lbs (900 grms)	3 lbs (1.58 kg)
Onions	8 oz (225 grms)	12 oz (340 grms)	1 lb (450 grms)
Leeks	1 small	1 medium	1 large
Carrots	3 large	4 large	5 large
Vegetable root	1 small	1 medium	1 large
Boiling water	2 pints (1.14 litres)	3 pints (1.7 litres)	4 pints (2.28 litres)
Salt	2 level teaspoons	1 tbl	1½ tbls
Sugar	½ teaspoon	1 teaspoon	1 lump

Pepper to taste

Place chicken pieces and giblets in deep bowl and cook on full power for 15 (20) (24) minutes until it comes to the boil. Remove scum and add vegetables and seasoning and cook on medium power for 45 (55) (60) minutes. Allow to cool a little and then strain. When cold remove fat and adjust seasoning. A little boiling water may be added to soup when reheating as the soup will be very concentrated.

CORN CHOWDER

Bondia Zimmerman

Preparation 10 minutes   Advance   Freezable

	2 servings	*4 servings*	*6 servings*
Onion chopped	1 medium	1 large	1½ large
Butter	¾ oz (21 grms)	1½ oz (42 grms)	2½ oz (71 grms)
Plain flour	1½ tbls	3 tbls	4½ tbls
Parsley chopped	1 tbl	2 tbls	3 tbls
Potato peeled and diced	4 oz (113 grms)	8 oz (225 grms)	12 oz (340 grms)
Turmeric	½ teaspoon	1 teaspoon	1½ teaspoons
Nutmeg	pinch	¼ teaspoon	½ teaspoon
Boiling water	12 fl oz (340 ml)	1¼ pints (¾ litre)	2 pints (1.14 litres)
Smoked haddock skinned and cubed	4 oz (113 grms)	8 oz (225 grms)	12 oz (340 grms)
Sweetcorn frozen or tinned	4 oz (113 grms)	8 oz (225 grms)	12 oz (340 grms)
Vegetable stock cubes	1	2	3
Salt and black pepper to taste			

Place butter in large bowl and cook on full power for 40–50 seconds until butter has melted. Add onion and potato and turn them over in the butter until they are coated. Cover bowl with pricked cling film and cook in microwave oven on full power for approximately 2 minutes. Stir in the spices and allow to stand for 3 minutes while you dissolve the cubes in the boiling water. Gradually add the stock to the contents of the bowl, stir in the fish and corn. Cover with pricked cling film and cook again for 4 (6) (9) minutes, stirring twice during cooking time. Serve with hot crusty bread.

COURGETTE SOUP

Preparation 10 minutes   Advance   Freezable

	2 servings	*4 servings*	*6 servings*
Courgettes finely chopped	¼ lb (113 grms)	½ lb (225 grms)	¾ lb (340 grms)
Garlic crushed	¼ teaspoon	½ clove	1 clove
Shallots finely chopped	2	3	4
Basil dried	¼ teaspoon	½ teaspoon	1 teaspoon
Margarine/Butter	½ oz (14 grms)	¾ oz (21 grms)	1 oz (28 grms)
Oil	½ teaspoon	¾ teaspoon	1 teaspoon
Vegetable stock cubes or parve beef cubes	½	1	2
Boiling water	¾ pint (425 ml)	1¼ pints (710 ml)	1¾ pints (1 litre)
Salt	½ teaspoon	¾ teaspoon	1 teaspoon
Parsley chopped	¾ tbl	1½ tbls	2 tbls
Black pepper to taste			

Garnish
1 tbl Parmesan cheese grated (optional)

Place oil, courgettes, shallots and garlic together in a large bowl. Cover with pricked cling film and cook for 3 (4) (5) minutes on full power. Add stock, basil and pepper, stir and cook covered for another 5 minutes. Melt butter/margarine and stir in parsley with the salt. Gradually add parsley mixture to soup. Reheat if necessary. Serve hot sprinkled with the Parmesan cheese (optional).

CHILLED CUCUMBER AND CHEESE SOUP

Preparation 5 minutes   Advance

	2 servings	4 servings	6 servings
Gouda cheese grated	4 oz (113 grms)	6 oz (170 grms)	8 oz (225 grms)
Onion chopped	½ small	1 small	1 medium
Oil	2 teaspoons	1 dessertspoon	1 tbl
Dried mixed herbs	2 teaspoons	1 dessertspoon	1 tbl
Cucumber peeled and chopped	1	1½	2½
Lemon juice	1 tbl	1½ tbls	2 tbls
Parve chicken broth	¼ pint (140 ml)	7 fl oz (200 ml)	12 fl oz (340 ml)
Salt and freshly ground black pepper to taste			

Place the oil and onion in a bowl. Cover with pricked cling film and microwave on full power for 1½ (2) (2¾) minutes. Purée onion with the cheese, cucumber, lemon joice, herbs, broth, salt and pepper. Stir in onion mixture. Chill thoroughly.

CREAMY CUCUMBER SOUP   Rosanna Burr

Preparation 10 minutes   Advance

	2 servings	4 servings	6 servings
Cucumber peeled	1 medium	1 large	1½ medium
Parve chicken stock or vegetable cubes	1	2	3
Boiling water	1 pint (570 ml)	1½ pints (850 ml)	2½ pints (1.42 litres)
Onion finely chopped	¾ teaspoon	1 teaspoon	1½ teaspoons
Butter	¾ oz (21 grms)	1 oz (28 grms)	1½ oz (42 grms)
Single cream	2 tbls	¼ pint (140 ml)	½ pint (284 mls)
Plain flour	½ oz (14 grms)	¾ oz (21 grms)	1 oz (28 grms)
Salt and pepper to taste			

Garnish
1 tbl mint finely chopped
1 tbl cucumber peel chopped

Cut the cucumber into small pieces and place in a large bowl with the stock and onion. Cook on full power for 5–7 minutes until the cucumber is soft and then purée or sieve it. Place butter in large bowl and microwave on full power for 30 (45) (60) seconds. Stir in the flour and then gradually stir in the puréed mixture. Season to taste and cook for another 3½ (4) (5) minutes. Stir in the cream. Allow to cool and refrigerate. Garnish with a little chopped mint mixed with chopped cucumber peel.

FRUIT SOUP
Lady Jakobovits

Serves 6   **Preparation 5 minutes**   **Advance essential**   **Freezable**

2 lbs (900 grms) **fresh fruit (mainly berries)**   **2 tbls potato flour**

Place washed fruit in a large pyrex dish and pour in enough water to come up to the same level. Cook on full power until it comes to the boil, remove any scum. Continue to cook on full power with the fruit boiling for 5 minutes, stirring occasionally. Simmer on defrost power for another 10 minutes. Allow to cool a little, then gently stir in the potato flour and cook for another 2 minutes on defrost power. Taste and add a little sugar if required. Chill for 24 hours before serving.

LEEK AND COURGETTE SOUP
Gillian Burr

Preparation 20 minutes   **Advance**   **Freezable**

	2 servings	*4 servings*	*6 servings*
Medium leeks thinly sliced	1	1½	2 large
Courgettes thinly sliced	**1 lb** (450 grms)	**1¼ lbs** (563 grms)	**2 lbs** (900 grms)
Margarine	½ tbl	¾ tbl	1 tbl
Watercress washed	½ bunch	¾ bunch	1 bunch
Olive oil	½ tbl	¾ tbl	1 tbl
Chicken stock boiling	**1 pint** (570 ml)	**1½ pints** (850 ml)	**2¼ pints** (1300 ml)

Salt and freshly ground black pepper to taste

Garnish
A few reserved watercress leaves

Place the sliced courgettes in a sieve and sprinkle with salt. Leave them to drain for 10 minutes. Discard any thick watercress stalks. Place leeks, courgettes, margarine and oil in a large bowl. Cook for 3 minutes on full power stirring once during the cooking time. Add the stock. Cover the bowl with pricked cling film and cook on full power for 2 minutes, then reduce to ¾ power for 4 (5) (6) minutes. Add the watercress and cook on full power for 1 (1½) (2) minutes. Purée the soup and then sieve it. Adjust seasoning and serve garnished.

LETTUCE SOUP
Lesley Levy

Preparation 5 minutes

	2 servings	*4 servings*	*6 servings*
Onion finely chopped	1 small	1 medium	1 large
Butter	1 oz (28 grms)	2 oz (56 grms)	3 oz (85 grms)
Plain flour	½ oz (14 grms)	1 oz (28 grms)	2 oz (56 grms)
Parve chicken stock	¼ pint (140 ml)	¾ pint (425 ml)	1 pint (570 ml)
Milk	¼ pint (140 ml)	½ pint (284 ml)	¾ pint (425 ml)
Lettuce leaves chopped	4 oz (113 grms)	8 oz (225 grms)	1 lb (450 grms)
Grated nutmeg	a pinch	¼ teaspoon	½ teaspoon
Caster sugar	a pinch	¼ teaspoon	½ teaspoon
Egg yolk	half	1 small	1
Freshly ground black pepper and salt to taste			

Place onion and butter in bowl, cover with pricked cling film and cook on full power for 4 minutes. Stir in flour, then gradually stir in hot stock, milk, lettuce, nutmeg, salt and pepper, cover again and cook on full power for 9 minutes. Cool slightly, then pour into blender with egg yolk and blend until smooth. Return soup to bowl, cover again and reheat for two minutes, stirring once or twice. Serve with croûtons.

MUSHROOM SOUP

Preparation 15 minutes   Advance

	2 servings	*4 servings*	*6 servings*
Mushrooms sliced	6 oz (170 grms)	12 oz (340 grms)	1 lb (450 grms)
Parsley chopped	½ tbl	1 dessertspoon	1 tbl
Margarine	½ tbl	1 dessertspoon	1 tbl
Onion finely chopped	1 small	1 medium	1 large
Garlic cloves crushed	1	1½	2
Soy sauce	1 tbl	1½ tbls	2 tbls
Boiling water	¾ pint (455 ml)	1¼ pints (720 ml)	2 pints (1 litre)
Single cream	1½ fl oz (1½ tbls)	2 fl oz (2¼ tbls)	3 fl oz (4 tbls)
Vegetable cubes crumbled	1	1½	2
Black pepper to taste			

Garnish
Chopped parsley

Place margarine in large bowl and microwave on full power for approximately 30 seconds until melted. Add onion and garlic and cook for 3 minutes. Add boiling water, parsley, mushrooms, soy sauce, stock cubes and pepper. Cover with pricked plastic film and cook on full power for 4½–5 minutes until the mushrooms are tender. Leave to cool. Purée the soup. Reheat the soup until very hot. Stir in cream and sprinkle with chopped parsley.

CREAM OF MUSHROOM SOUP   Sally Friend

Preparation 15 minutes   Advance

	2 servings	4 servings	6 servings
Button mushrooms thinly sliced	½ lb (225 grms)	¾ lb (340 grms)	1 lb (450 grms)
Butter	¾ oz (21 grms)	1½ oz (42 grms)	2 oz (56 grms)
Flour	½ oz (14 grms)	¾ oz (21 grms)	1 oz (28 grms)
Onion chopped	1 small	1 medium	1 large
Milk	½ pint (284 ml)	¾ pint (425 ml)	1 pint (570 ml)
Single cream (optional)	1 tbl	2 tbls	¼ pint (114 ml)
Salt and black pepper to taste			

Place butter in bowl and cook on full power for 30 seconds until it has melted. Add mushrooms and stir into butter, cook on full power for 40 seconds and then stir in the flour. Cook for 20 seconds, gradually add the milk stirring it until it has been absorbed. Season the soup. Cover the bowl with pricked cling film and cook on ¾ power for 9 (10) (12) minutes until mushrooms are soft but not mushy. Add cream just before serving and adjust seasoning to taste.

ONION SOUP   Bettina Bradfield

Preparation 10 minutes   Advance

	2 servings	4 servings	6 servings
Onions sliced	½ lb (225 grms)	1 lb (450 grms)	1½ lbs (675 grms)
Plain flour	½ oz (14 grms)	1 oz (28 grms)	1½ oz (42 grms)
Butter	½ oz (14 grms)	1 oz (28 grms)	1½ oz (42 grms)
Sugar	a pinch	½ teaspoon	1 teaspoon
Gruyère cheese grated	2 oz (56 grms)	3 oz (85 grms)	5 oz (142 grms)
Parmesan cheese grated	2 oz (56 grms)	3 oz (85 grms)	5 oz (142 grms)
White wine	2 fl oz (3 tbls)	3½ fl oz (5 tbls)	5 fl oz (140 ml)
Gravy browning	½ teaspoon	¾ teaspoon	1 teaspoon
Parve beef or vegetable stock	1 pt (½ litre)	2 pints (1¼ litres)	3 pints (1¾ litres)
French bread thinly sliced cut in half	1 slice	2 slices	3 slices
Salt and black pepper to taste			

Melt butter in an oval casserole dish and heat on full power until melted (30 seconds approximately). Add onions and stir well, cover and cook on full power for 3 (3½) (4½) minutes. Stir in flour, sugar, salt and pepper. Add stock and gravy browning ensuring that they are well mixed. Cook on full power covered with well pricked cling film for 15 (17) (20) minutes. Sprinkle on a third of the cheese. Float half slices of bread on top and cover with rest of cheese then either place dish back in microwave oven and cook on full power for 1 (1¼) (1½) minutes or place under hot grill until cheese is browned.

POTAGE ST. GERMAIN

Preparation 10 minutes		Advance	Freezable
	2 servings	*4 servings*	*6 servings*
Leeks roughly chopped	2 small	2 medium	3 large
Butter	1½ oz (42 grms)	2¼ oz (63 grms)	3¼ oz (90 grms)
Spring onions chopped	1	2	3
Lettuce, Iceberg or Cos chopped	½	1	1½
Frozen peas	1 lb (450 grms)	1½ lbs (675 grms)	2 lbs (900 grms)
Parve chicken stock	1 pint (½ litre generous)	1½ pints (1 litre scant)	2¼ pints (1 litre generous)
Lemon juice	1 teaspoon	1½ teaspoons	2 teaspoons
Curry powder	2 teaspoons	1 dessertspoon	1 tbl
Sugar	a pinch	½ teaspoon	1 teaspoon
Flour	1 tbl	1½ tbls	2½ tbls
Salt and pepper to taste			

Garnish
Mint, coriander or a few small peas

Sweat the leeks in butter for 3 (3½) (4) minutes. Add spring onions, lettuce and lemon juice. Cook on full power for 1¼ (1½) (2) minutes. Add curry powder, stir in flour and then add stock, peas, sugar, salt and pepper. Cook on full power for 10 (12) (15) minutes. Garnish with a few small peas, mint or coriander.

DUTCH VEGETABLE SOUP
Caroline Young
Anchor Hocking MicroWare

Serves 4–6 **Preparation 5 minutes** **Cook 15 minutes**

4 oz (110 grms) **onion skinned and finely chopped**
10 oz (280 grms) **frozen mixed vegetables**
4 chicken stock cubes
8 oz (225 grms) **smoked sausages sliced**

4 oz (110 grms) **quick cooking macaroni**
Salt and freshly ground black pepper to taste
3 pints (1.7 litres) **boiling water**
MicroWare simmer cooker

Combine onion and vegetables in the MicroWare simmer cooker. Dissolve the stock cubes in the boiling water and stir in. Cover and bring to the boil on full power – about 5 minutes. Stir in macaroni, cover and cook on full power for 7 minutes. Add sausage, stir, cover and let stand for 5 minutes. Season to taste. (See illustration page 66)

SUMMARY VEGETABLE SOUP

Preparation 10 minutes   Advance   Freezable without garnish

	2 servings	*4 servings*	*6 servings*
Spring onions chopped	**4**	**6**	**8**
Watercress			
coarsely chopped	**½ bunch**	**1 bunch**	**1½ bunches**
Chopped spinach			
fresh or frozen	**4 oz** (113 grms)	**8 oz** (225 grms)	**12 oz** (340 grms)
Petits pois frozen	**2 oz** (56 grms)	**4 oz** (113 grms)	**6 oz** (170 grms)
Fresh mint chopped	**½ tbl**	**1 tbl**	**1½ tbls**
Vegetable stock	**¾ pint**	**1 pint**	**1¾ pints**
	(½ litre scant)	(½ litre generous)	(1 litre)
Grapefruit juice	**2 fl oz** (3 tbls)	**5 fl oz** (140 ml)	**8 fl oz** (226 ml)
Oil	**1 tbl**	**2 tbls**	**3 tbls**

Garnish
Mint sprigs
½ cucumber peeled and cubed

Place vegetables, except mint, with oil in large bowl. Cover with pricked cling film and cook on full power for 6 minutes. Stir in the stock, cover and cook again on full power for 4½ (6) (8) minutes. Purée the soup and stir in grapefruit juice and mint. Season to taste and cook on full power for 4 minutes. Serve hot or chilled, garnished.

NOTES

FISH

HINTS

Fish tastes better when cooked in a microwave oven. It should be cooked on full power until the fish can be flaked.

Always cover fish before cooking in a microwave oven.

Do not reheat cooked fish in a microwave oven as it will become tough.

Place fish so that thickest parts of the fish are nearest the outside of the dish.

A good way of cooking fish in a microwave oven is to reduce some white wine on full power, pour it over the fish and then cook the fish on full power.

If cooking fish with a sauce – add the sauce half way through the cooking time.

If cooking a very thick piece of fish turn it over half way through the cooking time.

Fish carries on cooking during the standing time given in recipes, and will therefore stay hot whilst you are preparing a sauce to serve with it, or cooking some vegetables.

When cooking a very thick fish with a skin, it is a good idea to cut one or two slits in the skin to allow the steam made during cooking to escape.

When cooking fish fillets, fold a thin tail piece under so that the fish has an even thickness all over.

Do not try to deep fry in a microwave oven.

BREAM WITH ALMOND BUTTER

Preparation 5 minutes

	2 servings	4 servings	6 servings
Bream fillets	2	4	6
Butter	2 tbls	4 tbls	5 tbls
Lemon juice	2 tbls	4 tbls	5 tbls
Cornflour	1½ tbls	2 tbls	3 tbls
Toasted chopped almonds	¼ lb (113 grms)	½ lb (225 grms)	¾ lb (340 grms)
Salt	¼ teaspoon	½ teaspoon	¾ teaspoon
Black pepper	a pinch	¼ teaspoon	½ teaspoon
Parsley finely chopped	¾ tbl	1½ tbls	2 tbls

Melt the butter in a bowl on full power for 30–40 seconds, then stir in the cornflour and lemon juice which have been made into a smooth paste, add the parsley, salt, pepper and the almonds. Coat both sides of each fillet with the mixture and place the fillets in a shallow dish so that the thickest parts of the fish are nearest the outside of the dish. Cover with pricked cling film and cook on full power for 7 (8) (10) minutes until the fish is cooked. Allow to stand for 2 minutes before serving.

COD IN MUSHROOM SAUCE   Anna Larking

Preparation 5 minutes

	2 servings	4 servings	6 servings
Cod skinned	1 lb (450 grms)	1¾ lbs (790 grms)	2½ lbs (1.125 kg)
Condensed mushroom soup	1 tin	1½ tins	2 tins
Butter	1 oz (28 grms)	2 oz (56 grms)	3 oz (85 grms)
Worcestershire sauce	2 teaspoons	3 teaspoons	4 teaspoons
Cheddar cheese grated	4 oz (113 grms)	8 oz (225 grms)	12 oz (340 grms)
Salted crisps	1 small packet	1 small packet	1 large packet
Garlic salt and black pepper to taste			

Place fish in bottom of dish, cover with the soup. Sprinkle with the grated cheese. Cook on full power for 6 minutes. In a separate bowl, melt the butter on full power for 30 (40) (50) seconds, add the Worcestershire sauce and garlic salt and crisps. Spread the mixture over the top of the fish and cook on full power for 1 (1¼) (1¾) minutes.

FISH IN A CLAY POT

Serves 4   **Preparation 20 minutes**   **Cook 45 minutes approximately**

8 pint (4.5 litres) **unglazed clay pot**
3 lbs (1.35 grms) **fish, head and tail removed**
1½ tbls fennel chopped
1½ tbls leeks sliced very thinly
1½ tbls radish chopped

3 tbls butter
2 wine glasses dry white wine
1 small garlic clove
8 (approximately) sorrel or spinach leaves
Salt and pepper to taste

Soak the clay pot in cold water for 20 minutes. Soak the sorrel or spinach leaves in hot water for 10 minutes. Mix the fennel, leeks and radishes with the crushed garlic and a little salt and pepper and stuff the cavity of the fish with it. Tie it with fine string to keep the stuffing in position. Wrap the drained leaves around the fish. Place fish on inverted saucers or plates in the pot. Melt the butter in a small bowl on full power for 30 seconds, stir in the wine and then pour the mixture over the fish. Place lid on top and cook on full power until centre of fish will flake when tested with a fork, 40–50 minutes. Serve with juices.

FISH PIE

Preparation 5 minutes

	2 servings	*4 servings*	*6 servings*
Smoked haddock	¾ lb (340 grms)	1 lb (450 grms)	1½ lbs (675 grms)
Mushrooms thickly sliced	2 oz (56 grms)	3 oz (85 grms)	4 oz (112 grms)
Hard boiled eggs chopped	1½	2	3
Cooked mashed potato	¾ lb (340 grms)	1 lb (450 grms)	1¼ lbs (563 grms)
Parsley or cheese sauce	¼ pint (140 ml)	½ pint (284 ml)	¾ pint (425 ml)
Butter	½ oz (14 grms)	1 oz (28 grms)	1½ oz (42 grms)
Water	2 tbls	4 tbls	6 tbls

Place fish in a shallow dish with the water. Cover with pricked cling film and cook on full power for 4 (5) (6) minutes. Allow to cool, then flake the fish and mix it with the mushrooms, eggs, sauce and place in dish. Cover with the potato which has been mashed with the butter, spooning or piping it over the mixture. Cook in a microwave oven uncovered on full power for 6 (7) (8) minutes.

HADDOCK DELICIEUX   Valerie Joels

Preparation 5 minutes

	2 servings	4 servings	6 servings
Haddock filets	1 lb (450 grms)	1½ lbs (675 grms)	2½ lbs (1.125 kg)
Butter	½ oz (14 grms)	1 oz (28 grms)	1½ oz (42 grms)
Lemon	¼	½	1 small
Cream	2 tbls	4 tbls	6 tbls
Garnish: **Parsley chopped** ½ tbl		1 tbl	1½ tbls

Grease a suitable dish. Wash and dry the fish and cut into portions. Lay the fish in the greased dish and season. Moisten with the lemon juice and spoon over the cream. Cover with thickly buttered paper. Cook in a microwave oven on full power for 4 (5) (6) minutes. Garnish with chopped parsley.

HADDOCK AU GRATIN   Sally Friend

Preparation 15 minutes

	2 servings	4 servings	6 servings
Haddock fillets	8 oz (225 grms)	1 lb (450 grms)	1½ lbs (675 grms)
Smoked haddock fillets	4 oz (113 grms)	8 oz (225 grms)	12 oz (340 grms)
Bay leaf	1 small	1 medium	1 large
Onion thinly sliced	1 small	1 medium	1 large
Black peppercorns	3	6	9
Button mushrooms sliced	2 oz (55 grms)	4 oz (113 grms)	6 oz (170 grms)
Plain flour	1½ tbls	3 tbls	4½ tbls
Butter	1 oz (28 grms)	2 oz (56 grms)	3 oz (85 grms)
Cheddar cheese grated	1½ oz (42 grms)	3 oz (85 grms)	4½ oz (125 grms)
Dry white wine	2 tbls	4 tbls	6 tbls
Breadcrumbs fresh	½ oz (15 grms)	1 oz (28 grms)	1½ oz (42 grms)
Walnuts	½ oz (15 grms)	1 oz (28 grms)	1½ oz (42 grms)
Water	¼ pint (140 ml)	½ pint (284 ml)	¾ pint (425 ml)
White pepper to taste			

Place the fish in a shallow dish and cover with the wine and water. Add the peppercorns, onion and bayleaf. Cover with pricked cling film and cook on full power for 4½ (5) (6) minutes. Remove the fish, flake it and reserve. Strain the liquid into a jug. Place the butter in a dish that is suitable to be placed under a grill and melt the butter on full power for 30–40 seconds approximately. Stir in the mushrooms and cook on full power for 50 (60) (90) seconds. Stir in the flour and cook on full power for another 30 seconds. Stir in the reserved liquid and cook on full power for 5–6 minutes until boiling, stirring every minute. Stir in the fish with half the cheese and pepper to taste. Cook on full power for 1¾ (2) (2½) minutes. Mix the breadcrumbs, walnuts and the rest of the cheese together and sprinkle them over the fish in an even layer. Brown under a hot grill.

HADDOCK PROVENÇAL

Gillian Burr

Preparation 5 minutes

	2 servings	*4 servings*	*6 servings*
Haddock or cod cutlets, 6 oz (170 grms) **each**	2	4	6
Onion peeled and sliced	1 small	1 medium	1 large
Oil	1 tbl	2 tbls	3 tbls
Tomatoes peeled and sliced	2	4	6
Green peppers sliced	1	2	3
Mushrooms sliced	2 oz (56 grms)	4 oz (112 grms)	6 oz (170 grms)
Black olives pitted	1 oz (28 grms)	2 oz (56 grms)	3 oz (85 grms)
Fresh mixed herbs	¼ teaspoon	½ teaspoon	¾ teaspoon
Edam cheese grated	2 oz (56 grms)	4 oz (113 grms)	6 oz (170 grms)
Lemon juice	1 tbl	2 tbls	3 tbls
Salt and freshly ground pepper to taste			

Place fish in a shallow dish and cover with pricked cling film and cook on full power for 5 (6) (7) minutes and leave to stand. Place oil in a bowl with the onions, peppers, tomatoes and mushrooms, stir and cook covered on full power for 3 minutes stirring once during that time. Mix in the olives, lemon juice, herbs and seasoning and spread over the fish in an even layer. Sprinkle with the cheese and cook uncovered on full power until the cheese melts, 2–3 minutes, approximately. If the dish is suitable, the topping may be browned under a hot grill.

HADDOCK WITH RICE AND ORANGE SAUCE

Preparation 5 minutes

Freezable

	2 servings	*4 servings*	*6 servings*
Haddock fillets skinned	2	4	6
Onion thinly sliced	1 small	1 medium	1 large
Paprika	a pinch	¼ teaspoon	½ teaspoon
Water	10 fl oz (284 ml)	1 pint (568 ml)	1½ pints (0.85 litre)
Orange peel grated	½ orange	1 orange	1½ oranges
Walnuts or mixed nuts chopped	1 oz (28 grms)	2 oz (56 grms)	3 oz (85 grms)
Long grain rice	4 oz (113 grms)	8 oz (225 grms)	12 oz (340 grms)
Butter	1 oz (28 grms)	2 oz (56 grms)	3 oz (85 grms)

Place half the butter in a large shallow dish and cook uncovered for 30–60 seconds until it melts. Add the nuts, peel, water, salt and rice and cover with pricked cling film. Cook on full power for 14 (15) (19) minutes. Place the fish on top of the rice and cover with the onion rings. Dot with the remaining butter and sprinkle with a little paprika. Cover again with pricked cling film and cook on full power for 7 (8) (9) minutes. Leave to stand for 2–3 minutes.

BUTTERED SMOKED HADDOCK

Preparation 15 minutes

	2 servings	4 servings	6 servings
Smoked haddock	¾ **lb** (340 grms)	1¼ **lbs** (575 grms)	1¾ **lbs** (790 grms)
Butter	¼ **oz** (7 grms)	½ **oz** (14 grms)	1 **oz** (28 grms)
Cayenne pepper to taste			

Soak smoked haddock in cold water for 15 minutes and then drain. Put the smoked haddock in a dish that just fits. Dot with butter. Cook on full power for 3–4 minutes, until the flesh flakes easily. Serve garnished with a sprinkling of cayenne pepper.

CHEESY SMOKIES

Preparation 15 minutes

	2 servings	4 servings	6 servings
Smoked haddock skinned	4 **oz** (113 grms)	8 **oz** (225 grms)	12 **oz** (340 grms)
White sauce	¼ **pint** (140 ml)	½ **pint** (284 ml)	¾ **pint** (425 ml)
Cheddar cheese grated	1 **oz** (28 grms)	2 **oz** (56 grms)	3 **oz** (85 grms)
Plain yoghourt	1½ **tbls**	3 **tbls**	4½ **tbls**
English mustard, made	½ **mustard spoon**	1 **mustard spoon**	1½ **mustard spoons**
Black pepper to taste			

Garnish: **A few parsley sprigs**

Combine the white sauce and yoghourt then cut the fish into cubes and stir them into the sauce. Season with pepper and stir in half the cheese and the ready made mustard. Divide the mixture between individual ramekin dishes and sprinkle with the rest of the cheese or cook in 1 large dish. Cook uncovered on full power for 4 (5) (6) minutes until the fish is cooked through. Garnish with parsley.

HALIBUT FLORENTINE

Gillian Burr

Preparation 5 minutes

	2 servings	4 servings	6 servings
4 oz (112 grms) **halibut steaks**	**½ lb** (227 grms)	**1 lb** (450 grms)	**1½ lbs** (675 grms)
Butter	**¼ oz** (7 grms)	**½ oz** (14 grms)	**¾ oz** (21 grms)
Frozen spinach chopped	**4 oz** (113 grms)	**8 oz** (227 grms)	**12 oz** (340 grms)
Lemon juice	**1 teaspoon**	**1 dessertspoon**	**1 tbl**
Nutmeg grated	**a pinch**	**¼ teaspoon**	**a large pinch**
Tomato thinly sliced	**1 small**	**1 medium**	**1 large**
Cheese sauce ready made	**¼ pint** (140 ml)	**½ pint** (284 ml)	**¾ pint** (425 ml)
Salt and black pepper to taste			

Place the halibut steaks in a shallow dish with the thickest parts of the steaks to the outside of the dish, sprinkle with lemon juice and dot with butter. Cook on full power for 4 (5) (6) minutes, then carefully remove the bones. Place the spinach in a bowl, cover with pricked cling film and microwave on full power for 6 (7) (8) minutes, stirring twice during cooking. Drain the spinach thoroughly and season with salt, pepper and a little nutmeg. Spoon the spinach onto a serving dish and place the halibut steaks on top of it. Place a slice of tomato on each piece and pour over the cheese sauce. Cook on full power until hot. If the dish you are using is suitable to go under a hot grill you can cover the sauce with soft breadcrumbs and grated cheese and place under the hot grill until it browns.

HALIBUT AND SMOKED SALMON PARCELS

Pat Fine

Preparation 2 hours

	2 servings	4 servings	6 servings
8 oz (225 grms) **halibut**	**2**	**4**	**6**
Smoked salmon slices	**2**	**4**	**6**
Butter	**2 oz** (56 grms)	**4 oz** (113 grms)	**6 oz** (170 grms)
Milk to cover			
Lemon juice	**2 tbls**	**4 tbls**	**6 tbls**
Greaseproof paper	**4 pieces**	**8 pieces**	**12 pieces**
Salt and black pepper to taste			
Hollandaise sauce already made (see Sauce section)			

Soak salmon in milk for 2 hours, then drain it. Butter one piece of greaseproof paper for each piece of halibut. Season the halibut and then cover each piece with a slice of smoked salmon and place on a piece of greaseproof paper and wrap. Place on plate and microwave on full power for 5 (6) (7) minutes approximately. Serve with Hollandaise sauce, new potatoes and a green vegetable.

LEMON SOUSED HERRINGS

Preparation 10 minutes	Refrigeration 2 hours		Advance	Freezable
	2 servings	*4 servings*	*6 servings*	
Herrings each				
½ lb (225 grms)	2	4	6	
Mace	½ blade or pinch	1 blade	1½ blades	
Bay leaf	½	1	1½	
Peppercorns	3	6	9	
Cloves	½	1	1½	
Salt	small pinch	¼ teaspoon	½ teaspoon	
Water	2½ fl oz (75 ml)	¼ pint (140 ml)	7 fl oz (225 ml)	
Onion sliced	1 small	1 medium	1 large	
Lemon juice	⅛ pint (75 ml)	¼ pint (140 ml)	⅓ pint (225 ml)	

Ask your fishmonger to bone and remove the heads from the fish. Roll each one up, skin outside, from head end to the tail and arrange in a fairly deep dish. Sprinkle over the rest of the ingredients. Cover with pricked cling film and cook on full power for 5 (6) (7) minutes. Allow the fish to cool in the liquor, then refrigerate for 1–2 hours before serving.

MUSTARD HERRINGS

Preparation 5 minutes

	2 servings	*4 servings*	*6 servings*
Herrings gutted and			
cleaned	2	4	6
Mustard Dijon	3 teaspoons	1½ tbls	2¼ tbls
Flour	1 tbl	2 tbls	3 tbls
Butter	½ oz (14 grms)	1 oz (28 grms)	1½ oz (42 grms)
Lemon juice	1 tbl	2 tbls	3 tbls
Salt	½ teaspoon	1 teaspoon	1½ teaspoons

Place the butter in a dish just large enough to take the herrings side by side. Cook it for 30 seconds approximately until it has melted. Stir in the mustard, salt and lemon juice. Coat the herrings with the flour on both sides and place in the dish. Turn them over so that both sides of the fish are buttered. Cover with a piece of greaseproof paper and microwave on full power for 3 (3 minutes 40 seconds) (4) minutes until the fish is tender. Turn the fish over once during the cooking time.

KEDGEREE   Rosanna Burr

Preparation 15 minutes

	2 servings	4 servings	6 servings
Smoked haddock	**6 oz** (170 grms)	**12 oz** (340 grms)	**1¼ lbs** (565 grms)
Butter	**¾ oz** (21 grms)	**1½ oz** (42 grms)	**2 oz** (56 grms)
Long grain rice cooked	**1⅓ cups**	**2½ cups**	**3½ cups**
Hard boiled eggs chopped	**1**	**2**	**3**
Single cream	**2 tbls**	**4 tbls**	**6 tbls**
Parsley chopped	**1 tbl**	**2 tbls**	**3 tbls**
Cayenne pepper	**a pinch**	**¼ teaspoon**	**½ teaspoon**
Paprika	**¼ teaspoon**	**½ teaspoon**	**¾ teaspoon**

Soak the fish for a few minutes in cold water to remove excess salt, then put the fish in a deep dish and place a few small dots of butter on it. Cover with pricked cling film and cook on full power for 2½ (3½) (5) minutes until the fish is cooked. Flake the fish and remove skin. Drain the juice. Place the rest of the butter in the still hot dish and stir until melted, add the fish, chopped egg and rice and stir again. Cover once more and cook on full power for 3½ (4½) (5½–6) minutes, until the rice is piping hot. Stir in the cream. Sprinkle with the parsley, cayenne pepper and paprika.

MARINATED CITRUS MACKEREL   Anne Larking

Preparation 3 hours

	2 servings	4 servings	6 servings
Mackerel fillets	**2**	**4**	**6**
Orange rind grated	**½ orange**	**1 orange**	**1½ oranges**
Lemon rind grated	**½ lemon**	**1 lemon**	**1½ lemons**
White wine vinegar	**1 tbl**	**2 tbls**	**3 tbls**
Oil	**1 tbl**	**2 tbls**	**3 tbls**
Sugar	**1 teaspoon**	**2 teaspoons**	**3 teaspoons**
Marmalade	**3 tbls**	**6 tbl**	**9 tbls**
Salt and pepper to taste			

Garnish: **Orange slices, bay leaves**

Marinate mackerel fillets for 2–3 hours at least, in the vinegar, oil, rinds and seasonings. Strain the juices into a bowl and stir the marmalade into them. Cook on full power for 1½ minutes to dissolve the marmalade. Spoon over the fish. Cover the bowl with pricked cling film, cook for 7–8 (8–9) (10–11) minutes on full power until cooked. Garnish with orange slices and bay leaf. Serve hot or cold with a mixed salad.

PLAICE WITH RHUBARB AND ORANGE SAUCE   Anne Moss

Preparation 20 minutes

	2 servings	*4 servings*	*6 servings*
Plaice fillets, small, skinned and boned	4	8	12
Butter	½ oz (14 grms)	1 oz (28 grms)	1½ oz (42 grms)
Sauce			
Rhubarb	4 oz (113 grms)	8 oz (225 grms)	12 oz (340 grms)
Oranges, squeezed	1½	3	4
Coarse cut marmalade	1 tbl	2 tbls	3 tbls
Cayenne pepper	a pinch	¼ teaspoon	½ teaspoon
Salt and freshly ground black pepper to taste			

Roll the fillets up carefully. Grease a shallow dish with half the butter and place the fish in it. Dot the fish with the remaining butter, cover with greaseproof paper and cook on full power for 5 (5½) (6) minutes, until fish is tender.

Sauce:
Trim and wash the rhubarb and slice into ½ inch (1 cm) pieces and place in a bowl. Pour the orange juice over it, add the marmalade, salt, black pepper and cayenne pepper. Cook on full power for 1½ (2) (2½) minutes approximately until it comes to the boil. Stir once and then cook on half power until the mixture is tender and the liquid has reduced to become a syrupy sauce. Pour over the fish and serve hot.

PLAICE FILLETS WITH SPINACH LASAGNE

Serves 6   Preparation 10 mins.   Cook 25 mins.   Standing time 8 mins.

Filling
1 large onion sliced
1¼ lbs white fish fillets (563 grms)
1 tbl plain flour
¼ pint fish stock (140 ml)
1 small tin tomatoes
2 tbls tomato purée
3 tbls parsley chopped
1 tbl lemon juice
3 oz Cheddar cheese grated (85 grms)
Pinch nutmeg
6 oz lasagne verde (170 grms)

Topping
2 oz Parmesan cheese (56 grms)

Sauce
1 pint milk (570 ml)
1 oz carrot sliced (30 grms)
1 stick celery sliced
1 small onion sliced
4 parsley sprigs
Strip of lemon rind
4 black peppercorns
3 tbls plain flour
2 oz butter
3 fl oz white wine (85 ml)
Salt and pepper to taste

Sauce: Place milk in a large bowl with the parsley, lemon rind, celery, onions, carrot and peppercorns. Cook on full power until the milk comes to the boil, 6 minutes approximately. Remove and leave to stand for 10 minutes. Melt butter in a bowl on full power for 30 seconds and stir in the flour. Cook on high for another minute, then gradually stir in the wine. Strain the milk and stir it into the wine mixture until it is smooth. Cook on full power for another 2 minutes, beat well and cook again for another minute. Repeat. The sauce should now have thickened. Adjust the seasoning.

Filling: Place fish and onion in a shallow dish and cover with pricked cling film. Cook on high for 6 minutes. Flake the fish. Grease a 3½ pint (2 litre) shallow dish. Blend the flour with a little of the stock and then add the tomatoes, tomato purée, parsley, lemon juice and seasoning. Mix the fish into it. Place one-third of the lasagne in the bottom of the dish and cover with half the fish mixture, then more lasagne and then the sauce sprinkled with some of the grated cheese and nutmeg. Repeat in layers, finishing with sauce. Cover with pricked cling film and cook on full power for 8 minutes. Leave to stand for 8 minutes. Sprinkle the top with the Parmesan cheese and brown under a medium hot grill.

LIME AND GINGER SALMON

Preparation 10 minutes

	2 servings	*4 servings*	*6 servings*
Salmon steaks	2	4	6
Butter	1 tbl	2 tbls	3 tbls
Lime slices	4	8	12
Ginger root chopped	½ tbl	1 tbl	1½ tbls

Garnish: **Lime wedges**

Place salmon steaks in a shallow dish with thickest parts towards the outside of the dish. Cover with the butter and ginger root which have been processed together until smooth. Top with the lime slices and cover with pricked cling film and microwave on full power for 4 (5) (6) minutes. Allow the fish to stand for 4 minutes.

SALMON MOUSSE WITH WATERCRESS SAUCE Gloria Smith

Serves 4   Preparation 10 minutes   Cook 15 minutes

Salmon mousse
8 oz (225 grms) **salmon**
1 **egg**
1 **tbl fish stock**
  (see page 85)
2 oz (56 grms) **cream cheese**
Salt and freshly ground black pepper

Sauce
½ oz (14 grms) **butter**
2 oz (56 grms) **onion finely chopped**
2 **tbls watercress finely chopped**
5 fl oz (142 ml) **fish stock**
3 fl oz (85 ml) **double cream**
4 **buttered ramekins**
Garnish
Sprigs of watercress

Salmon mousse: Place all ingredients in a food processor and blend until smooth and creamy. Divide the mixture between the ramekins. Cover loosely with pricked cling film. Cook on defrost power, No.3, for 10–12 minutes until just set. Keep warm.

Sauce: Melt the butter on high. Cook for 30 seconds, stir in onion and cook on full power for 1½ minutes. Add the watercress, stock and the cream and cook uncovered on full power for 1–2 minutes until slightly reduced. Unmould the salmon mousses onto heated plates and spoon the sauce over them. Garnish with watercress.

SAUMON EN PAPILLOTE

Preparation 7 minutes

	2 servings	4 servings	6 servings
Salmon steaks	2	4	6
Pimento chopped	2 tbls	4 tbls	6 tbls
Broccoli spears, frozen	½ lb (225 grms)	1 lb (450 grms)	1½ lbs (665 grms)
Tartare sauce	1½ tbls	2½ tbls	4 tbls
Plain flour	¾ tbl	1 tbl	2 tbls
Dried dill weed	a pinch	¼ teaspoon	½ teaspoon
Lemon juice	1½ teaspoons	1 dessertspoon	1 tbl
Chopped parsley	½ teaspoon	1 teaspoon	2 teaspoons
Condensed cream of onion soup	½ tin	1 tin	2 tins
Greaseproof or bakewell paper, cut in squares			
Paprika to taste			
Salt and black pepper to taste			

Butter each piece of greaseproof paper and leave buttered side up. Place broccoli spears and pimento on each corner. Cover each with a salmon steak. Place soup, sauce, dill weed and lemon juice with the flour in a bowl, mix well and then spoon over the pieces of fish. Sprinkle with paprika and the chopped parsley. Fold each piece of paper over to make a triangle and to enclose the fish steak. Fold the edges over to seal. Place the parcels on a flat plate and microwave on full power for 6 (7) (8) minutes and then leave to stand for 3 minutes before serving with new potatoes.

POACHED SALMON STEAKS

Gillian Burr

Preparation 5 minutes

	2 servings	4 servings	6 servings
Salmon steaks	2	4	6
Onion sliced	1 small	1 medium	1 large
Carrot	1	2	3
Celery	½ stick	1 small stick	1 large stick
White wine/Lemon juice	1 tbl	2 tbls	3 tbls

Salt and black pepper to taste

Place salmon steaks in a suitable sized dish side by side, with the thickest part of the slice to the outside of the dish. Season and then pour over the wine/lemon juice. Place the vegetable slices around the fish. Cover with pricked cling film and cook on full power for 4 (5) (6) minutes. Leave to stand for 3–4 minutes as the fish will continue to cook during the standing time.

SALMON RISSOLES

Preparation 5 minutes

Advance

	2 servings	4 servings
Red salmon tinned	4 oz (113 grms)	8 oz (225 grms)
Mashed potato	4 oz (113 grms)	6 oz (170 grms)
Onion chopped	1 small	1 medium
Butter	1 teaspoon	2 teaspoons
Lemon juice	1 teaspoon	2 teaspoons
Parsley chopped	1 tbl	2 tbls
Egg beaten	1 small	1 large
Breadcrumbs/Fine matzo meal	4–5 tbls	8 tbls
Vegetable oil	3 tbls	6 tbls

Salt and black pepper to taste

Drain and flake the salmon. Add potato, butter, lemon juice and parsley and mix thoroughly. Season to taste. Add the beaten egg and stir it in. Shape the mixture into equal portions and roll them into the breadcrumbs, pressing them in. (If you have a browning dish, place it in the oven and heat on full power for 7 minutes, then add oil and rissoles, press down, turn them over and press again until they have a good colour, continue to cook for 3 (4) minutes.) Place the oil in a dish and cook on full power for 1 minute. Put the rissoles in the dish side by side as near the outside of the dish as possible. Cover the rissoles with some kitchen paper and microwave on full power for 3 (4) minutes. Drain well on kitchen paper and serve either hot or cold with a salad.

MARINATED SALMON TROUT   Miki Hildebrand

Serves 6–8   **Preparation 5 minutes**   **Advance**

4 lbs salmon trout cleaned (1.8 kg)
2 tbls butter
1 small onion chopped
2 teaspoons fresh tarragon or
   1 teaspoon dried tarragon
Grated rind from ½ lemon

¼ pint dry white wine (142 ml)
½ iceberg lettuce shredded
Salt and pepper to taste

Garnish: **Cucumber slices**
          Lemon slices
          Mayonnaise

Make several deep slits along the length of the trout skin in order to allow the steam to escape during cooking. Place the butter in a small bowl with the onion, and cook on full power for 2½ minutes. Stir in the tarragon, lemon rind and seasoning to taste. Spoon this mixture into the body cavity of the fish. Place in a shallow dish and pour the wine over the fish. Cover and cook on full power for 18–20 minutes. Allow the fish to cool in the dish and then remove the skin. Place the fish on a platter on a bed of shredded lettuce and decorate with cucumber slices, lemon slices and mayonnaise.

SAVOURY STUFFED FISH

Preparation 5 minutes

	2 servings	*4 servings*	*6 servings*
Trout, gutted, cleaned and scaled	2	4	6
Lemon rind grated	½ lemon	1 lemon	1½ lemons
Lemon juice	½ lemon	1 lemon	1½ lemons
Stuffing			
Soft breadcrumbs	1 dessertspoon	1½ tbls	2½ tbls
Parsley chopped	1 tbls	2 tbls	3 tbls
Butter	2 tbls	4 tbls	6 tbls
Nutmeg	¼ teaspoon	½ teaspoon	1 teaspoon
Salt	½ teaspoon	1 teaspoon	1½ teaspoons
Pepper	¼ teaspoon	½ teaspoon	1 teaspoon
Egg	1 small	1 large	2 small

Garnish: **Sliced cucumber and lemon**

Squeeze the lemon juice over the inside cavity of the fish. Melt the butter in a bowl and cook on full power for 30 seconds, add the rest of the stuffing ingredients and mix thoroughly. Fill the fish cavities with the stuffing and secure the edges with wooden toothpicks or tie them up. Place the fish in pricked oven bags and cook for 4 (5) (6) minutes until cooked. When cooked, the fish should flake easily. Serve hot garnished with the cucumber and lemon.

GREEK FISH
Anne Moss

Serves 4   **Preparation 5 minutes**

5 lbs sea bass, gutted, cleaned and scaled
   (2 kgs 250 grms)
Juice from 1 lemon
7 tbls olive oil
1 large onion, finely sliced
2 cloves garlic, crushed
2 celery sticks, chopped

3 carrots, chopped
15 oz tin tomatoes (425 grms)
7 tbls dry white wine
½ teaspoon sugar
Salt and pepper to taste
Garnish
Parsley sprigs and lemon butterflies

Wash a dry fish. Squeeze lemon juice over the fish and season with salt and pepper. In a large casserole place the oil, onion and garlic, celery and carrot and cook on full power for 3 minutes. Place the fish on top of the vegetables and cover with the wine and tomatoes. Sprinkle with the sugar. Cover and cook on full power for 15 minutes approximately until the fish is cooked. Allow to stand for 2 minutes before serving. Garnish.

HERB STUFFED SEA BASS WRAPPED IN LETTUCE
Gillian Fenner

Serves 4–6   **Preparation 10 minutes**   **Cook 12 minutes**

1½ lbs sea bass boned and cleaned
   (675 grms)
2 large round lettuce
1–2 oz butter (28–56 grms)
2 tbls shallots finely chopped
2 tbls dry vermouth
4 fl oz dry white wine (114 ml)
4 fl oz double cream (114 ml)

Stuffing
8 oz chopped spinach parboiled (225 grms)
2 oz fine breadcrumbs (56 grms)
1 oz butter softened (28 grms)
2 oz sorrel leaves finely shredded (56 grms)
1 teaspoon tarragon finely chopped
1 egg beaten
Salt and pepper to taste
2 oz parsley finely chopped (56 grms)

Place 20 large lettuce leaves in a bowl, add salt and blanch with boiling water so as not to damage leaves, drain carefully and then pour cold water over them. Place each one carefully on a towel to dry.

Stuffing: Mix spinach, breadcrumbs and butter, mash well and then stir in the rest of the ingredients. Stuff the fish firmly and reform into original shape. Place shallots in bottom of shallow dish. Salt and pepper the fish and wrap it (except the head) in the lettuce leaves, pressing them firmly into place. Place in the dish. Dribble the dry vermouth over the fish, add the white wine and dot with butter. Cover with buttered greaseproof paper and cook on full power for 10 minutes, basting two or three times during the last 5 minutes. Transfer fish to serving dish and leave covered to stand while finishing off the sauce. Cook the juices left in the dish on full power until reduced to a little syrup. Stir in the cream and cook again until reduced by half. Whisk in 1 oz (28 grms) of butter, pour the sauce over the fish and serve.

45

TROUT IN ALMONDS

Preparation 5 minutes

	2 servings	4 servings	6 servings
Trout	2	4	6
Lemon juice	1 teaspoon	2 teaspoons	3 teaspoons
Butter	1 oz (28 grms)	2 oz (56 grms)	3 oz (85 grms)
Almonds split	1 oz (28 grms)	2 oz (56 grms)	3 oz (85 grms)
White pepper	1 pinch	¼–½ teaspoon	½–¾ teaspoon
Salt to taste			

Garnish: **Parsley sprigs and lemon wedges**

Place almonds and butter in a shallow dish and cook uncovered on full power until they are golden brown, 5 minutes approximately. Remove the almonds with a slotted spoon and reserve. Place the trout in the dish, turning them over to ensure that both sides are coated in the butter. Sprinkle with a little salt. Add pepper and chopped parsley and lemon juice. Cover with pricked cling film and cook on a low power for 6 (7) (8) minutes. Remove the cling film and sprinkle the almonds over the fish. Cover again and cook on low power for another minute. Leave to stand for 2 minutes before serving garnished.

NB: A nice variation is to substitute chopped hazelnuts for the almonds, cooked in the same way.

TROUT WITH LEMON AND CREAM   Helen Paiba

Preparation 3 minutes

	2 servings	4 servings	6 servings
Trout washed and dried	2	4	6
Oil	1 tbl	2 tbls	3 tbls
Lemon slices	2	4	6
Single cream	2 tbls	4 tbls	6 tbls
Salt and black pepper to taste			

Pour oil into a suitable dish. Add seasoning and cook on full power for 1 minute. Place trout in dish and turn the fish so that it is oiled on both sides. Place a lemon slice on the top of each trout. Pour the cream over them. Cover with pricked cling film, place in the oven and cook on full power for 4 (5) (6) minutes. Allow to stand for 3–4 minutes before serving.

MEAT

HINTS

Browning dishes   are particularly useful when cooking meat dishes as the surface sears the food in the same way as when you fry or grill it, and at the same time browns the meat. Meat cooks so quickly in a microwave oven that it does not have time to get brown – a browning dish rectifies this.

Roasts   are most successful if cooked without a bone.

should be raised on a trivet when cooked so that they do not sit in their own juices. These may be used to made gravy with at the end of the cooking time.

should be left to stand wrapped in a foil tent for 15–20 minutes at the end of the cooking time. The joint will, in fact, still be cooking even though it is out of the oven.

BEEF

SURPRISE BURGERS
Jane Finestone

Serves 4–6   **Preparation 5 minutes**   **Cook 15 minutes**

2 lbs (900 grms) **lean beef steak finely minced**
Salt and black pepper to taste

Sauce (optional)
2 tbls tomato purée
¼ cup red wine
Fresh basil
Black pepper to taste

Filling
1 lb (450 grms) **frozen leaf spinach**
3 cloves garlic crushed
Black pepper to taste
Browning dish
N.B. If you do not have a browning dish sear the burgers in a frying pan.

Filling: Defrost the spinach on defrost power for about 4 minutes. Squeeze out most of the water. Mix it with the crushed garlic and lots of black pepper.

Salt the meat and form into beef burgers pushing a large lump of the spinach and garlic into the centre and closing the hole with some more mince meat.

Heat your browning dish according to the manufacturer's instruction for about 7 minutes and then sear the burgers in the dish. Then cover them with a lid and cook on power level 7 or ¾ power for 15 minutes, leaving them to stand for 4 minutes. The alternative is to sear them in a frying pan and then cook them in the sauce in the microwave oven.

BEEF CASSEROLE

Preparation 5 minutes	Advance	Freezable
	4 servings	*6 servings*
Lean stewing beef cubed	**1 lb** (450 grms)	**1½ lbs** (675 grms)
Plain flour	**1 level tbl**	**1½ level tbls**
Mixed frozen vegetables	**½ lb** (225 grms)	**¾ lb** (340 grms)
Beef stock	**½ pint** (284 ml)	**¾ pint** (425 ml)
Salt	**½ teaspoon**	**¾ teaspoon**
Pepper	**a pinch**	**½ teaspoon**
Onion sliced	**1 medium**	**1 large**

Heat oil in shallow dish with onion on full power for 2 minutes. Add meat in a single layer, sprinkle the flour over it and turn it over in the oil. Mix in the vegetables. Cover with pricked cling film and cook on full power for 15 minutes. Add stock, seasoning and stir again. Cook on medium power for another 15 (17) minutes.

CHILLI CON CARNE

Preparation 10 minutes   *Freezable*

	2 servings	*4 servings*	*6 servings*
Lean minced beef	**1 lb** (450 grms)	**1½ lbs** (675 grms)	**2 lbs** (900 grms)
Onion finely chopped	**1 medium**	**1 large**	**1½ medium**
Clove garlic finely crushed	**2**	**3**	**4**
14 oz tin tomatoes chopped and drained (400 grms)	**1**	**1½**	**2**
Tomato purée	**4 tbls**	**8 tbls**	**12 tbls**
Chilli powder	**1 rounded tbl**	**1½ rounded tbls**	**2 rounded tbls**
Can red kidney beans drained, 15 oz (425 grms)	**1**	**1½**	**2**
Salt to taste			

Garnish: **Thin slices of green pepper**

Place mince in a large shallow dish. Add garlic and onion. Fork thoroughly. Cook uncovered on high power for 5 (6) (7) minutes. Stir. Add rest of the ingredients except the kidney beans. Cover with pricked cling film, and cook for 15 minutes on medium power, stirring occasionally. Add kidney beans, stir well and cook on medium power for 10 (12) (15) minutes. Leave to stand for 5 minutes. Garnish with green pepper. Serve with rice or crusty bread and green salad.

MARINATED BEEF CURRY

Preparation 5 minutes   **Marinating time 2 hours minimum**

	2 servings	*4 servings*	*6 servings*
Topside of beef lean and cubed	**¾ lb** (340 grms)	**1¼ lbs** (563 grms)	**2 lbs** (900 grms)
Onion finely chopped	**1**	**2**	**3**
Cloves of garlic crushed	**1**	**2**	**3**
Coriander	**1 tbl**	**2 tbls**	**3 tbls**
Ginger	**½ teaspoon**	**1 teaspoon**	**1½ teaspoons**
Turmeric	**½ teaspoon**	**1 teaspoon**	**1½ teaspoons**
Chilli powder	**½ teaspoon**	**1 teaspoon**	**1½ teaspoons**
Cumin	**½ teaspoon**	**1 teaspoon**	**1½ teaspoons**
Cider vinegar	**2 fl oz** (60 ml)	**4 fl oz** (114 ml)	**6 fl oz** (170 ml)
Water	**4 fl oz** (114 ml)	**8 fl oz** (225 ml)	**12 fl oz** (340 ml)
Oil	**1 tbl**	**1½ tbls**	**2 tbls**
Salt	**¾ teaspoon**	**1½ teaspoons**	**2 teaspoons**
White pepper	**a pinch**	**¼ teaspoon**	**½ teaspoon**

Blend coriander, turmeric, ginger, cumin and chilli powder with the garlic and onion, and place in a deep bowl. Add the vinegar and mix until it forms a paste. Add the meat, cover and leave to stand for at least 2 hours or overnight in the refrigerator. Heat oil and water in a 3 pint (1½ litre) dish on full power for 1½ (2) (2½) minutes. Add the meat with all its juices, spices, etc. Season with salt and pepper and cook on medium power for 35 (40) (43) minutes. Leave to stand for 7 minutes before serving. Serve with hot rice and chutney.

GOULASH

Pat Fine

Preparation 10 minutes   Advance   Freezable

	2 servings	4 servings	6 servings
Chuck steak cubed	¾ lb (340 grms)	1½ lbs (675 grms)	2¼ lbs (1 kg)
Plain flour	1 tbl	2 tbls	3 tbls
Oil	1 tbl	2 tbls	3 tbls
Onions finely sliced	1	2	3
Green pepper deseeded and chopped	1 small	1 medium	1 large
Tinned tomatoes drained	7 oz (200 grms)	14 oz (400 grms)	1½ lbs (663 grms)
Cloves garlic crushed	1	2	3
Tomato purée	1½ tbls	3 tbls	4½ tbls
Paprika	1 tbl	1 heaped tbl	1½ heaped tbls
Water	¼ pint (140 ml)	½ pint (284 ml)	¾ pint (425 ml)
Salt and pepper to taste			
Parsley			

Heat oil in a large shallow dish. Dust meat with flour. Add meat, onions, pepper and garlic to oil. Stir well. Cover with lid or pricked cling film. Microwave on full power for 15 minutes. Add tomatoes, purée, paprika and water. Stir and recover. Cook on low power for 35 (40) (45) minutes stirring occasionally. Serve with noodles sprinkled with poppy seeds.

ROAST RIB OF BEEF

Serves 8   **Preparation 8 minutes**   **Cook 29 minutes**   **Stand 15 minutes**

Rib of beef, 4 lbs (1.8 kg)   Bay leaf
Large onion sliced   Dry mustard
Large carrot sliced   Browning dish

Heat empty browning dish on full power for 8 minutes. While it is heating, rub the mustard into the meat and sprinkle with pepper. Place meat in dish and press into dish, turn on each side until it is all sealed and slightly brown, then ensure that the meat is left with the fatty side up and cook on full power for 6 minutes, brush any melted fat over all sides of the meat and add onion and carrot plus 1 tbl of water on the bottom of the dish. Continue to cook on half power for 8 minutes, turn meat over and continue to cook on half power for another 15 minutes. Cover with foil and leave to stand for 15 minutes (the meat continues to cook during the standing time). Meat cooked in this way will be medium rare.

SPICY MEATBALLS

Preparation 10–15 minutes   Makes 30 small meatballs

8 oz (225 grms) **minced beef**   8 oz (225 grms) **minced veal**
2 tbls plain flour   1 tbl tomato purée
1 egg beaten   ½ teaspoon paprika
1 tbl grated onion   A pinch ginger

Heat a browning dish on full power for 5 minutes. Mix the meat with the rest of the ingredients and shape into small balls. Place 1 tablespoon of oil in dish, add as many meatballs as the dish will hold keeping them in one layer. Cook uncovered on full power for 2 minutes. Turn the meatballs over and cook for a further 2 minutes. Repeat with remaining meatballs. Serve hot with drinks or with a barbecue sauce. Delicious served on a bed of rice for a buffet dish.

SHEPHERD'S PIE   Goldie Allan

Preparation 15 minutes   Advance   Freezable

	2 servings	*4 servings*	*6 servings*
Onion thinly sliced	1 small	1 medium	1 large
Carrots grated	1 large	2 medium	2 large
Vegetable oil/Dripping	1½ tbls	2 tbls	3 tbls
Lean minced beef	¾ lb (340 grms)	1¼ lbs (565 grms)	2 lbs (900 grms)
Worcestershire sauce	½ tbl	¾ tbl	1 tbl
Brown sauce	½ tbl	¾ tbl	1 tbl
Tomato purée	½ tbl	¾ tbl	1 tbl
Mushroom ketchup	½ tbl	¾ tbl	1 tbl
Water boiling, to cover			
Salt, pepper and mixed herbs to taste			

Topping

Potatoes	¾ lb (340 grms)	1¼ lbs (565 grms)	2 lbs (900 grms)
Nutmeg	a pinch	a pinch	¼ teaspoon
Breadcrumbs	1 tbl	2 tbls	3 tbls
Telma margarine			
Salt and pepper to taste			

Place oil in casserole and heat on full power for 1 minute, add onion and grated carrot and cook for another minute. Add the meat and stir until brown. Cover with boiling water, tomato purée, sauces, seasoning and herbs, stir. Cook uncovered on full power until it comes to the boil. Cover with pricked cling film and cook on medium power for 22 (25) (30) minutes. Cover with mashed potatoes. Sprinkle the breadcrumbs over the potato and brown under a hot grill or reheat in microwave oven on full power.

SPAGHETTI BOLOGNESE

Preparation 5 minutes

	2 servings	4 servings	6 servings
Minced beef	½ lb (225 grms)	¾ lb (340 grms)	1 lb (450 grms)
Onion chopped	1 small	1 medium	1 large
Clove garlic crushed	1 small	1 medium	1 large
Tin tomatoes	¼ lb (113 grms)	½ lb (225 grms)	1 lb (450 grms)
Green pepper chopped	½	1 small	1 medium
Tomato purée	¾ teaspoon	1¼ teaspoons	2 teaspoons
Worcestershire sauce	¾ teaspoon	1¼ teaspoons	2 teaspoons
Oregano	¾ teaspoon	1¼ teaspoons	2 teaspoons
Beef cube	¼	½	1
Salt	1 pinch	½ teaspoon	1 teaspoon
Black pepper to taste			
Long spaghetti	5 oz (145 grms)	10 oz (285 grms)	1 lb 2 oz (500 grms)

Mix meat with onions, garlic and pepper and place in a large shallow bowl. Cook uncovered on full power for 3 (4) (5) minutes. Add tinned tomatoes, purée, oregano, Worcestershire sauce and crumbled stock cube. Mix well with fork. Cook covered with pricked cling film on medium power for 22 (26) (30) minutes mixing once or twice with a fork. Leave to stand for 5 minutes. Serve with spaghetti cooked as per packet instructions.

BEEF STEW WITH DUMPLINGS

Preparation 10 minutes   Advance   Freezable

	2 servings	4 servings	6 servings
Lean braising steak cubed	¾ lb (340 grms)	1½ lbs (675 grms)	2¼ lbs (1.13 kg)
Plain flour	1 tbl	2 tbls	3 tbls
Onion sliced	1 small	1 medium	1 large
Cloves garlic crushed	1 small	1 medium	1 large
Beef cube	½	1	1½
Bouquet garni	1	2	3
Carrots sliced	1	2	3
Tinned tomatoes drained	7 oz (200 grms)	14 oz (400 grms)	1¼ lbs (563 grms)
Potatoes cubed	1 medium	2 medium	3 medium
Water	¼ pint (140 ml)	½ pint (284 ml)	¾ pint (425 ml)
Salt and pepper to taste			
Dumplings			
Self raising flour	1 oz (28 grms)	2 oz (55 grms)	3 oz (85 grms)
Fresh parsley	1 teaspoon	2 teaspoons	3 teaspoons
Shredded beef suet	½ oz (15 grms)	1 oz (28 grms)	1½ oz (42 grms)
Salt and pepper to taste			

Stew: Mix flour, crumbled cube and seasoning and coat meat in the mixture. In casserole dish place rest of ingredients and mix well, add the meat. Cover with pricked cling film and cook on full power for 10 minutes. Stir the meat and cook on half power for 25 (30) (35) minutes.

Dumplings: Place the ingredients in a bowl and add enough water to make a soft dough. Turn onto a floured surface and roll into 2 (4) (6) dumplings. Add the dumplings to the meat and cook on half power for another 20 minutes. Remove the bouquet garni and allow to rest for 5 (6) (7) minutes before serving.

WINTER SPICY BEEF

Preparation 5 minutes   Advance   Freezable

	2 servings	*4 servings*	*6 servings*
Minced lean beef	½ lb (225 grms)	¾ lb (340 grms)	1 lb (450 grms)
Onion chopped	1 small	1 medium	1 large
Green pepper chopped	1 oz (28 grms)	2 oz (55 grms)	3 oz (85 grms)
Clove garlic crushed	½	1 small	1 medium
Raisins	2 oz (55 grms)	4 oz (113 grms)	6 oz (170 grms)
Pearl barley	2 oz (55 grms)	4 oz (113 grms)	6 oz (170 grms)
Oregano	¼ teaspoon	½ teaspoon	1 teaspoon
Ground cummin	¼ teaspoon	½ teaspoon	1 teaspoon
Chilli powder	1 tbl	1½ tbls	2 tbls
Parsley chopped	1 tbl	2 tbls	3 tbls
Tinned tomatoes	2 tbls	small tin	medium tin
Water	4 fl oz (142 ml)	6 fl oz (213 ml)	½ pint (284 ml)
Salt and pepper to taste			

Place the water in a bowl and add the barley with the chilli powder, cummin, oregano and juice from the tomatoes. Cover with pricked cling film and cook on full power for 12 (16) (20) minutes, stirring twice during the cooking time. Place the meat in a bowl with the onion, pepper and garlic and cover with pricked cling film and cook on full power for 3 (4) (5) minutes. Drain excess fat and then mix the meat with the barley mixture. Add the tomatoes, raisins, salt and pepper to taste. Cook on full power for 5 minutes. Allow to stand for 10 minutes before serving. Delicious stuffed into pitta bread for informal supper.

LAMB

CARRE D'AGNEAU

Preparation 5 minutes

4 thick lamb cutlets with 2 bones	**½ tbl vegetable oil**
2 tbls flour	**7 tbls hot chicken stock**
2 tbls clear honey	**½ teaspoon salt**
Freshly ground black pepper	**4 orange slices**

Garnish: **Fresh mint**

Place browning dish on full power for 5 minutes. Cut two horizontal slits in the meat down to the bone and place an orange slice in each slit. Place meat in dish and microwave uncovered on full power for 4 minutes turning meat over after 2 minutes. Mix rest of ingredients together and pour over meat. Cover with lid or pricked cling film and cook on low power for 10 minutes until the meat is tender. Leave to stand covered for 5 minutes. Garnish and serve hot.

CIDER LAMB

Serves 4–6 **Preparation 5 minutes** **Cook 45 minutes** **Freezable**

3½ lbs (1.58 kg) **shoulder of lamb, boned and cubed**
1 tbl **plain flour**
2 tbls **oil**
1 **red pepper deseeded**
1 **green pepper deseeded**

15 oz (425 grms) **can peaches or apricots in syrup**
4 **spring onions chopped**
¾ pint (455 ml) **dry cider**
4 oz (113 grms) **beansprouts**
Salt and pepper to taste

Mix oil and flour together in a deep casserole. Cook on full power until pale brown, add the cubed lamb and mix well, then cook on full power for another 5 minutes. Add rest of ingredients other than the beansprouts. Cover with pricked cling film and cook on medium power for 40 minutes, adding beansprouts 1 minute before end of cooking time. If required for a smaller number the rest will freeze beautifully.

ROAST CROWN OF LAMB

Serves 6–8 **Preparation 10 minutes** **Cook 45 minutes approximately**

Crown with 18 bones
1 teaspoon **dried rosemary**
1 teaspoon **celery salt**
Large onion sliced
Large carot sliced
Salt and pepper to taste
Garnish
Watercress sprigs
Cutlet frills
5 **halves peaches or apricots spiced** (see Preserve section for recipe)

Stuffing
8 oz (225 grms) **minced lamb**
2 **celery sticks thinly sliced**
1 **onion chopped**
4 oz (113 grms) **coarse breadcrumbs**
2 oz (56 grms) **raisins**
3 tbls **chopped parsley**
½ teaspoon **lemon rind grated**
2 oz (56 grms) **Telma margarine**
Salt and pepper to taste

Stuffing: Place meat in bowl uncovered and cook on full power for 5 minutes, stirring half way. At the same time, place onion, margarine and celery in a bowl, cover with pricked cling film and cook on full power for 4 minutes until 'al dente', mix with the remaining stuffing ingredients and the lamb. Rub the seasoning for the crown between the chops and all around it. Cook meat on a roasting rack. Allow 15 minutes per pound when cooking on half power but cook on full power for the first five minutes with the bones at the bottom of the dish and then on half power for the first half of the cooking time. Turn the meat over and fill the cavity with the stuffing which should be covered with pricked cling film for the rest of the cooking time. If using a probe, it should reach 75 C (175F). Leave the meat to stand for 10 minutes covered loosely with silver foil. To serve, place crown on a serving dish. Cover the ends of the bones with paper cutlet frills and place the watercress sprigs and spiced peaches or apricot halves around the crown.

LAMB FRICASSEE

Caroline Young
Anchor Hocking Micro Ware

Serves 6 Preparation 10 mins. Cook 35–40 mins. Advance until**

2½–3 lbs (1.13–1.36 kg) **shoulder of**
  lamb in 1 inch (2.5 cms) **cubes**
1 large onion finely sliced
2 tbls oil
2 tbls plain flour
1 vegetable stock cube
7 fl oz (200 ml) **boiling water**
7 fl oz (200 ml) **dry vermouth**

1 lb (450 grms) **frozen baby carrots**
2 egg yolks
½ **lemon rind**
2 tbls lemon juice
2 tbls parsley chopped
Salt and freshly ground black pepper
  to taste
Micro Ware Supreme casserole

Combine lamb, onion and oil in the casserole and cook on full power for 5 minutes stirring once. Stir in the flour. Dissolve the cube in the water and together with the vermouth pour it over the meat. Stir in thoroughly together with the carrots, cover and cook on full power for 25–30 minutes or until the lamb is just cooked. **

Beat together the egg yolks, lemon juice, rind and parsley plus 5 tbls of hot cooking liquid. Stir into the casserole, check the seasoning and cook on full power for 5 minutes, stirring once until just beginning to thicken. Leave to stand covered for 5 minutes. If cooked ahead to this point, bring back to the boil before continuing from **. See page 66 for photograph.

LAMB RISSOLES

Preparation 7–10 minutes

	2 servings	*4 servings*	*6 servings*
Cooked lamb	½ **lb** (225 grms)	**1 lb** (450 grms)	1½ **lbs** (675 grms)
Onion finely chopped	**1 small**	**1 medium**	**1 large**
Bread	1½ **slices**	**3 slices**	4½ **slices**
Tomato purée	**1 tbl**	**2 tbls**	**3 tbls**
Dried mint	**2 teaspoons**	**3 teaspoons**	**4 teaspoons**
Eggs	**1 small**	**1 medium**	**1 large**
Oil	**1 tbl**	**2 tbls**	**3 tbls**

Salt and pepper to taste
Four to coat
Mint jelly

Mince the lamb, onion and bread, season and add dried mint and tomato purée. Mix well and add beaten egg. Shape into rissoles. Coat well with flour. Place oil in dish and cook on full power for 1 minute. Add rissoles and turn them over half way through the cooking time. Cook on full power for 6 (10) (15) minutes. Move the inside rissoles half way through cooking to the outside of the dish. Serve with mint jelly.

SHOULDER OF LAMB WITH APRICOT STUFFING

Lynne Goldwyn

Serves 4   **Preparation 10 minutes**   Cook 1 hour 10 minutes

2 lbs (1 kg) shoulder of lamb boned	2 tbls oil
¾ lb (340 grms) veal minced	1 pint (568 ml) chicken stock
4 oz (113 grms) fresh white breadcrumbs	1 bouquet garni
3 onions peeled and sliced	15 oz (425 grms) can apricots drained
4 sticks celery chopped	Salt and black pepper to taste

Heat browning dish in oven on full power for 5 minutes. Chop half the apricots and mix with the veal, breadcrumbs and seasoning. Spread over the centre of the meat, then roll the meat into a Swiss roll shape and secure with string. Brush with the oil. Place the meat in the hot browning dish and turn over so that all sides are browned. Place the onions and celery around the meat with the bouquet garni and pour over the chicken stock. Cover with pricked cling film and cook on full power for 20 minutes. Turn the meat over, add the remaining apricots, cover the meat and cook on low power for 45 minutes until the meat is tender. Leave to stand covered for 5 minutes.

IRISH STEW

Preparation 10 minutes   **Advance**   **Freezable**

	2 servings	*4 servings*	*6 servings*
Lean stewing lamb cubed	¾ lb (340 grms)	1¼ lbs (563 grms)	2 lbs (900 grms)
Potatoes peeled and diced	¾ lb (340 grms)	1 lb (450 grms)	1½ lbs (675 grms)
Onions coarsely chopped	2 medium	2 large	3 large
Boiling water	¼ pint (140 ml)	½ pint (284 ml)	¾ pint (425 ml)
Salt	¾ level teaspoon	1 level teaspoon	1½ level teaspoons
Pepper to taste			
Garnish:			
Parsley chopped	1 level tbl	2 level tbls	3 level tbls

Place meat, onions and potatoes in a large shallow dish, cover with pricked cling film or a lid, cook for 12 (15) (19) minutes on full power. Mix salt and water together and pour them over the meat. Cover again and cook on ¾ power for 22 (25) (28) minutes. Allow to stand covered for 10 minutes and then garnish and serve.

WINTER WARMING LAMB

Preparation 15 minutes	Advance		Freezable
	2 servings	*4 servings*	*6 servings*
Middle neck of lamb sliced	1 lb (450 grms)	2 lbs (900 grms)	3 lbs (1.35 kg)
Flour	1 oz (28 grms)	2 oz (56 grms)	3 oz (85 grms)
Oil	1 tbl	2 tbls	3 tbls
Onions peeled and quartered	1	2	3
Small carrots peeled and sliced	5	7	12
Sticks celery sliced	1	2	3
Beef stock	½ pint (284 ml)	¾ pint (425 ml)	1 pint (570 ml)
Frozen peas	3 oz (85 grms)	4 oz (113 grms)	6 oz (170 grms)
Cauliflower florets	¼ head	½ head	¾ head
Salt and pepper to taste			

Heat a large browning dish on full power for 7 minutes and while it is heating, season the flour and toss the meat in it. Add the oil to the dish and cook on full power for 1 minute. Place the meat in the dish and turn it in the oil so that it is browned evenly. Cook on full power for 5 minutes. Add onions, celery and carrots and stock. Cover with pricked cling film or lid and cook for 30 (35) (40) minutes on medium power. Add the peas and cauliflower and cook on medium for another 8 (10) (13) minutes. Allow to stand for 10 minutes before serving.

VEAL

VEAL CASSEROLE

Preparation 10 minutes   Advance   Freezable

	2 servings	4 servings	6 servings
Stewing veal cubed	¾ lb (340 grms)	1¼ lbs (663 grms)	2 lbs (900 grms)
Margarine	1 tbl	2 tbls	3 tbls
Plain flour	1 tbl	2 tbls	3 tbls
Button mushrooms	2 oz (56 grms)	4 oz (113 grms)	6 oz (170 grms)
Chicken stock	8 fl oz (225 ml)	¾ pint (455 ml)	1¼ pints (710 ml)
Lemon juice	1 teaspoon	2 teaspoons	3 teaspoons
Dried basil	½ teaspoon	1 teaspoon	1½ teaspoons
Shallots blanched	2	4	6
Salt and pepper to taste			

Place margarine in a casserole and cook on full power for 30 seconds until melted, then add the veal, 1 (1½) (2) cups of stock, lemon juice, basil, salt and pepper and stir well. Cover with pricked cling film and cook on low for 20 (25) (29) minutes. Blend flour with remaining stock and mix with veal, add the onions and mushrooms. Cover and cook for a further 4 (8) (11) minutes until the veal is tender. If a thick sauce is desired stir a beaten egg yolk into the sauce and cook for a further minute on medium power.

PARTY VEAL MARENGO   Elissa Bennett

Serves 4–6   **Preparation 15 minutes**   **Cook 32 minutes**   Advance

2 lbs (900 grms) stewing veal cubed
1 lb (450 grms) pickling onions
  peeled but left whole
1 clove garlic crushed
½ lb (225 grms) button mushrooms
1 lb (450 grms) tomatoes
  skinned and chopped

Large pinch mixed dried herbs
10 fl oz (284 ml) dry white wine
4 tbls olive oil
Salt and pepper to taste
1 medium onion chopped
Garnish
1 tbl parsley chopped

Cooking on full power, sauté the mushrooms in the olive oil until just tender (about 1 minute) and then set aside. Sweat the pickling onions in the same oil and set aside. Then add the chopped onion and garlic to the oil, and sauté them and set aside. Lastly add the cubed meat to the oil and brown on all sides. Pour the wine into the dish and stir to scrape all the sediment at the bottom into the mixture. Stir in the chopped onion, garlic, tomatoes and herbs. Cover with a lid or pricked cling film and simmer on medium power until tender, 25–30 minutes. Season to taste and stir in the baby onions and mushrooms. Garnish. Leave to stand for 5 minutes. Serve with rice, new potatoes or croûtons. If you require a thicker sauce, stir 2 teaspoons cornflour which has been mixed with a little white wine into the dish 3 minutes before the end of the cooking time.

OFFAL

LIVER CASSEROLE

Preparation 5 minutes

	2 servings	4 servings	6 servings
Liver thinly sliced	½ lb (225 grms)	1 lb (450 grms)	1½ lbs (675 grms)
Large tomatoes thickly sliced	1	2	3
Oil or margarine	1 tbl	2 tbls	3 tbls
Flour	1 tbl	2 tbls	3 tbls
Mustard powder	¾ teaspoon	1 teaspoon	1¼ teaspoons
Stock or water	5 fl oz (142 ml)	8 fl oz (227 ml)	12 fl oz (341 ml)
Salt and pepper to taste			

Garnish
Chopped parsley

Heat oil or margarine in suitable dish for ½–1 minute. Mix flour, mustard, pepper and salt together and coat liver thoroughly with the seasoned flour. Place liver in dish and cook in a microwave oven on full power for 2 minutes on each side. Place tomatoes on liver, add stock and swirl around dish. Sprinkle with parsley. Cover loosely with kitchen paper and cook on medium power for 10 (15) (20) minutes.

OXTAIL   Gillian Fenner

Serves 6	Preparation 10 minutes	Cook 2 hours	Advance	Freezable

Oxtail cut in pieces
2 large onions peeled and sliced
1½ oz (42 grms) margarine
2 large carrots peeled and chopped
1 stick of celery chopped
1 turnip or swede peeled and chopped
6 black peppercorns

1 bay leaf
¼ pint (142 ml) red wine
Salt to taste
Garnish
2 tbls chopped parsley
Beurre manié made with 2 oz (56 grms)
margarine and 1 oz (28 grms) flour

Heat browning dish following the manufacturer's instructions and brown the oxtail in it. Add margarine and onions and cook on full power for 2 minutes. Transfer them to a large bowl and add remaining vegetables and seasoning, cover with water. Stir in the wine. Cook on full power until it comes to the boil and remove the scum. Cover with pricked cling film and cook on low heat for 1 hour, then medium heat for 45 minutes, adding more boiling water if the meat appears to be getting dry. Remove bay leaf and add the beurre manié in small pieces. Simmer on low heat until the sauce has thickened. Adjust seasoning and stir in chopped parsley.

POULTRY

HINTS

When you cook crumb-coated chicken pieces always place them on a microwave rack, so that the chicken does not stew in the pan juices. Do not turn the chicken pieces over as you may lose some of the crumbs.

To test if poultry is cooked, pierce the thickest part of the leg – the juices will run clear when the meat is cooked.

To defrost whole poultry, always place it on a microwave rack so that the bottom of the poultry does not start to cook in the pan juices. Poultry is first defrosted on 30% power and then on 10%. Finally leave to stand in cold water until completely defrosted.

Do not pack the stuffing too tightly in a bird as it will take so long to cook through that the rest of the bird will become overcooked.

CHICKEN CURRY
David Burr

Serves 4   **Preparation 10 minutes**   **Cook 28 minutes**   Advance

8 chicken portions small
1 tbl margarine
3 onions thinly sliced
2 stalks celery chopped
2 tbls corn oil (if frying)
1 green apple peeled and chopped
1 tomato chopped

1 green pepper sliced
1 clove garlic crushed
1 tbl plain flour
1–2 tbls curry powder
1 cup chicken stock
Browning dish

Garnish: **Shredded coconut**

Heat browning dish according to maker's instructions, about 7 minutes. Place the chicken portions in the dish and turn until browned on all sides. Remove the meat and leave aside. Place margarine in the browning dish and add onions, celery, apple, tomato and green pepper and cook on full power until softened – about 5 minutes. Add the garlic, then sprinkle the flour and curry powder over and cook on medium power, stirring frequently for 2 minutes. Stir in the stock and return the chicken to the browning dish. Cover with pricked cling film and cook on full power for 15 minutes when the chicken should be tender. Serve hot, garnished with the coconut and accompanied by rice and chutney. If you do not have a browning dish, fry the chicken in the oil on a conventional hob to brown it, and then continue with the recipe as above.

CHICKEN DHANSAK
Gillian Fenner

Preparation 5 minutes – soak lentils 12 hours   Advance   Freezable

	2 servings	*4 servings*	*6 servings*
Chicken portions skinned	2	4	6
Brown lentils ready to use	3 oz (85 grms)	6 oz (170 grms)	9 oz (255 grms)
Onions peeled and chopped	1 medium	2 medium	2 large
Tinned tomatoes	7½ oz (215 grms)	14 oz (397 grms)	20 oz (565 grms)
Potatoes peeled and sliced	1 medium	2 medium	2 large
Chilli powder	¼ teaspoon	½ teaspoon	¾ teaspoon
Ground turmeric	½ teaspoon	1 teaspoon	1½ teaspoons
Ground coriander	½ tbl	1 tbl	1½ tbls
Ground cummin seeds	½ teaspoon	1 teaspoon	1½ teaspoons
Chicken stock	¼ pint (140 ml)	½ pint (284 ml)	¾ pint (425 ml)
Lemon juice	½ lemon	1 lemon	1 large lemon
Margarine	½ oz (14 grms)	1 oz (28 grms)	1½ oz (42 grms)

Place chicken, lentils, vegetables, spices and half the stock in a large bowl, add the salt and cook on full power until it comes to the boil. Cover with pricked cling film and cook on low power for 15 (18) (22) minutes, until cooked and liquid has reduced. Remove the chicken from the bowl and cut into bite sized pieces. Purée the vegetables and lentils. Return them to the clean bowl and add the chicken, lemon juice and margarine. Reheat on low power adding more stock if the sauce is too thick; check seasoning. Serve with saffron rice, mango chutney, ground coconut and sultanas.

FRUIT STUFFED SPRING CHICKENS   Gloria Smith

Serves 2   Preparation 15 minutes   Cook 20 minutes   Standing time 8 minutes

2 x 1 lb spring chickens (450 grms)
1 medium onion chopped
4 oz dried apricots cooked (113 grms)
2 oz mushrooms (56 grms)

A handful walnuts chopped
Microwave seasoning to sprinkle
Chicken fat to dot
Salt and pepper to taste

Place chickens on a microwave trivet so that the juices will drain off during the cooking. Coarsely blend the onions, apricots, mushrooms and walnuts. Stuff the chicken with this mixture. Smear the chicken fat over the skins and sprinkle with microwave seasoning and salt and pepper. If there is any stuffing over, leave on one side. Cover chickens with domed lid or slit roaster bags and cook on No.7 (Roast) for 16 minutes. Place the chickens on a warm dish and cover tightly with foil for 8 minutes standing time.

Gravy: Take 2 tablespoons of the juice from the bottom of the trivet and stir into the remaining stuffing. Heat this in a small bowl loosely covered on full power for 3 minutes and serve as sauce with the chickens.

GALANTINE OF CHICKEN   Anna Larking

Serves 4   Preparation 30 minutes   Cook 15 minutes   Standing time 15 minutes

1 x 3 lb boned chicken (1.36 kg)
Stuffing
8 oz lean minced meat (225 grms)
1 small onion
1 teaspoon mixed herbs
Oil and margarine
Salt and pepper to taste

Rind and juice of ½ lemon
2 oz mushrooms chopped (56 grms)
½ beaten egg
A little chicken stock
6 olives stoned
1 stick celery chopped
A "J" cloth, string and a trussing needle

Place the minced meat, onion, herbs and seasoning in a bowl, mix in the lemon juice and rind, then the chopped mushrooms. Stir in the egg and enough chicken stock to give a firm, moist consistency. Place the stuffing in the middle of the chicken. Draw the long sides of the chicken over the stuffing and sew neatly together with fine string, forming the chicken into an even sausage shape. Heat the oil and margarine together and fry both sides of the chicken until golden brown. Take the chicken out of the pan and wrap it in a "J" cloth and tie the ends securely. (Greaseproof paper could be used.) Cook chicken on full power for 15 minutes. Wrap the chicken in foil very tightly and leave to stand for 15 minutes. Serve hot or cold.

SWEET GALANTINE OF CHICKEN — Anna Larking

Serves 4–6   Preparation 15 mins.   Cook 15 mins.   Standing time 15 mins.   Advance

3 lb chicken boned (1.36 kg)

Stuffing
6 oz sausage meat (170 grms)
3 oz dried apricots cooked and chopped
  (85 grms)
1½ tbls mint sauce
1 oz matzo meal (28 grms)
Juice and rind from 2 oranges

Juice from ½ lemon
A little chicken stock
½ egg
Salt and pepper to taste
Oil for frying (optional)
Browning dish (optional)
"J" cloth, string and needle

Mix all the stuffing ingredients until it has a moist consistency. Place it in the centre of the chicken and pull together the long sides and sew them neatly. Either heat the browning dish for about 7 minutes according to maker's instructions and then turn the chicken in it until all the sides are brown, or fry the chicken in the oil on a conventional hob. Tie chicken in a "J" cloth and then cook on full power for 15 minutes, turning it over half way through the cooking time. Wrap the chicken tightly in foil and leave to stand for 15 minutes. Serve hot or cold.

CHICKEN LEGS — Vada

Serves 6   **Preparation 2 hours**   **Cook 12 minutes**

16 small chicken legs
2 tbls honey
4 tbls soy sauce
4 tbls vinegar
2 tbls sherry or cognac

4 tbls chicken stock
4 tbls sugar
4 cloves garlic
Salt and pepper

Place the chicken legs in a large dish, cover with the rest of the ingredients and leave for at least 1½ hours. Cook on full power for 4 minutes, then turn the legs over and cook again for another 4 minutes; turn them over again and cook for the last 4 minutes. Can be browned under a grill.

DUCK

DUCK WITH APPLE SAUCE

Serves 4   **Preparation 10 minutes**   **Cook 8 minutes**

2 duck breasts
2 tbls clear honey
1 tbl walnut oil
1 tbl olive oil
4 fl oz (114 ml) white wine
2 Worcester Pearmain apples
Juice and grated rind of 1 lime

1 teaspoon cornflour
1 tbl cold water
1 teaspoon green peppercorns
Salt and freshly ground black pepper
  to taste
Large browning dish

Heat the browning dish on full power for 8 minutes or according to maker's instructions. Spread the honey over the duck portions and sprinkle with black pepper. Place the oil in the browning dish and the duck pieces skin side downwards. Cook on full power for 1 minute, then gently turn the duck pieces over. Add the rest of the ingredients *except* the cornflour and water and cook on full power for 5 minutes. Remove the duck pieces, slice them if required and then place them on a serving dish. Garnish with the apple slices and the peppercorns. Blend the cornflour into the water and then gradually stir the mixture into the sauce in the browning dish and cook on full power for 1½ minutes until the sauce has thickened. Pour a little of the sauce over the duck and serve the rest in a gravy boat. Serve with French beans or mange tout.

DUCK WITH GINGER SAUCE

Serves 4   **Preparation 10 minutes**   **Cook 35 minutes**

5 lb duck (2.27 kg)
1 orange sliced
1 large orange peel grated
¼ pint orange juice (142 ml)
2 lbs marmalade (900 grms)

Ginger sauce
1 tbl honey
2 teaspoons ground ginger
2 oz crystallized ginger chopped (56 grms)
1 teaspoon cornflour

Cover the tips of the wings, tail end and legs of the duck with a little foil to prevent them from being overcooked. Prick the skin of the duck well to allow the excess fat to drain. Glaze with the marmalade and top with the orange slices. Place in a split roasting bag on a microwave trivet. Cook on full power for 15 minutes. Drain off the fat and juices. Cook on full power for another 15 minutes. Wrap in foil and leave to stand for 10 minutes. Crisp under a hot grill just before serving.

Ginger sauce: Place all the ingredients except the cornflour in a jug and cook on full power for 3 minutes. Blend the cornflour with 1 tablespoon of cold water and stir into the sauce. Cook again on full power for 1 minute, stirring once, until the sauce has thickened.

DUCK WITH ORANGE SAUCE

Serves 3–4   **Preparation 10 minutes**   **Cook 45 minutes**

3¼ lb duck (1½ kg)
1 tbl tomato ketchup (optional)
Sauce
1 orange rind grated
¼ pint orange juice (150 ml)
¼ pint duck giblet stock (150 ml)

1 tbl cornflour
1 tbl sugar
1 tbl brandy/Cointreau
Salt and pepper to taste
Garnish: 2 slices of orange, halved

Tie the legs and wings of the duck securely to the body. Cover the ends of the legs with a little foil. Prick the duck well and place breast-side down on two saucers, upturned in a rectangular dish. Cook on full power for 12 minutes. Drain off the fat at the bottom of the dish and remove the foil. Turn the duck over, breast-side up, and brush with the ketchup if required. Cook on power 4 (low) for 15 minutes. Brush again with the ketchup, and cook on full power for 15 minutes. Remove from the oven, cover the duck tightly with foil and leave to stand.

Orange Sauce: Place the cornflour and orange rind in a bowl or jug. Mix to a smooth paste with the orange juice and stock. Add the sugar, salt and pepper and stir well. Cook on full power for 2 minutes. Whisk and then cook on full power for a further minute. Stir in the liqueur. Place the duck on a serving dish and pour half the orange sauce over it. Garnish the duck breast with the orange slices. Serve the remaining orange sauce separately.

TURKEY

TURKEY CASSEROLE   Railah Jason

Serves 4   **Preparation 10 minutes**   **Cook 19 minutes**

4 turkey fillets
Sauce
1 medium carrot sliced
1 stick celery finely chopped
1 medium onion finely chopped
2 oz button mushrooms sliced (56 grms)

1½ oz plain flour (42 grms)
1½ oz margarine (42 grms)
¾ pint hot chicken stock (426 ml)
1 tbl sherry
Salt and black pepper to taste
Browning dish large

This recipe is cooked on full power throughout. Place the browning dish on full power for 8 minutes or according to maker's instructions, then place the turkey fillets in it and turn them over so that they are seared on both sides. Cover with pricked cling film and cook for 5 minutes. Set aside. Place the vegetables with the margarine in a medium bowl and cook for 6 minutes, stirring the vegetables 2 or 3 times. Stir in the flour and then gradually add the stock and the sherry, stirring them well to ensure a smooth sauce. Season to taste and cook, covered, for 2 minutes, stirring once during this time. Pour the sauce over the turkey fillets and cook for another 5 minutes. Serve with green beans.

Dutch vegetable soup

Lamb Fricasée

CHEESY COURGETTE CASSEROLE

Preparation 5 minutes

	2 servings	*4 servings*	*6 servings*
Courgettes thinly sliced	4 oz (113 grms)	8 oz (225 grms)	12 oz (340 grms)
Onion chopped	1 small	1 medium	1 large
Tomatoes skinned and chopped	4 oz(113 grms)	8 oz (225 grms)	12 oz (340 grms)
Clove garlic crushed	1 small	1	1 large
Parsley chopped	1 teaspoon	2 teaspoons	1 dessertspoon
Red wine vinegar	½ tbl	1 tbl	1½ tbls
Cheddar cheese grated	2 tbls	4 tbls	6 tbls
Salt and black pepper to taste			

Place first seven ingredients in large bowl and stir well. Cover with pricked cling film and cook on full power for 11 (14) (17) minutes stirring half way through. Sprinkle with the cheese and cook uncovered on full power for 2–3 minutes until the cheese begins to bubble or if preferred brown under a medium hot grill.

POTATO AND SMOKED SALMON PUDDING   Phyllis Horal

Soaking time 8 hours   **Preparation 15 minutes**   **Cook 20 minutes**

6 oz smoked salmon (170 grms)   2 eggs
1½ lbs cooked skinned   1¾ oz butter (50 grms)
   new potatoes (677 grms)   ¼ pt single cream (142 ml)
1 finely chopped onion   Pepper
fresh dill (lots)

Soak salmon covered in milk and water for at least 8 hours. Slice potatoes thinly and lay over chopped onion in oven-proof dish. Spinkle with pepper and cover with the sliced salmon. Top with another layer of potatoes. Whip the egg and cream and pour over the dish. Cook on medium power for 20 minutes. This dish may also be cooked in a conventional oven but will take 1 hour on a low heat.

PARSNIPS AND CORN SUPREME

Preparation 8 minutes   **Cook 8 minutes**

1½ lbs parsnips peeled and   1 tbl fresh parsley
   quartered (677 grms)   Salt and pepper
4 oz frozen corn niblets (113 grms)   3 tbls water
½ oz butter/margarine (15 grms)

Place the water, salt and pepper in a large bowl. Add the parsnips, cover with pricked cling film and cook on full power for 4 minutes. Add the corn and parsley, cover again and cook for a further 4 minutes. Leave to stand covered for 3 minutes, strain and then stir in the butter. Serve immediately.

VEGETABLES

Vegetables	Vegetables cooked in a microwave oven need very little water and thus do not lose many vitamins.
Barbecued corn	To frozen corn add a little butter, 2 tbls of tomato ketchup and 6 drops of Worcestershire sauce. Cook in usual way.
Devilled corn	To frozen corn add 2 tbls of honey, 1 tbl of chopped basil and a few drops of Tabasco sauce and cook in the usual way.
Carrots	Cook 1 lb (450 grms) carrots with the juice and grated rind of 1 lemon, together with 2 tbls of brown sugar. Cover with pricked cling film and cook on full power for 15 seconds. Leave to stand for 5 minutes.
Aubergines	Cook sliced aubergines in a microwave oven on full power for 1 minute before frying. In this way they absorb far less oil than usual and are therefore less fattening.
Potatoes	Parboil your potatoes in the microwave oven on full power for 8 minutes before roasting in a conventional oven.

AUBERGINE AND POTATO

Preparation 1 hour

	2 servings	*4 servings*	*6 servings*
Aubergines thinly sliced	**½ lb** (225 grms)	**¾ lb** (340 grms)	**1 lb** (450 grms)
Potatoes thinly sliced	**3 oz** (85 grms)	**6 oz** (170 grms)	**8 oz** (225 grms)
Eggs	**1 small**	**1 large**	**2 large**
Milk	**2 fl oz** (60 ml)	**¼ pint** (140 ml)	**½ pint** (284 ml)
Mustard powder	**shake**	**pinch**	**¼ teaspoon**
Water	**1 tbl**	**2 tbls**	**3 tbls**
Salt and freshly ground black pepper			

Place the aubergines in a colander, sprinkle with salt and leave for 1 hour to sweat. Rinse salt off and pat dry. Place the potatoes and water in a shallow dish, cover with pricked cling film and cook on full power for 5 minutes until tender. Drain.

Sauce: Beat together eggs, milk, mustard, ¼ (½) (1) teaspoon salt and pepper to taste. Heat a browning dish on full power for 5–8 minutes add the butter and aubergine slices turn them over and then cook on full power 4 (5) (6) minutes, stirring half way through the cooking time. Place a layer of the potatoes on top and pour the sauce through a strainer over them. Cover and cook on low power for 3 (3½) (4) minutes. Stir the edges of the sauce for a second, then return to the oven and microwave uncovered for 4 (5) (6) minutes until the sauce has nearly set. Cover and leave to stand for 5 minutes before serving.

FRENCH BEANS

Preparation 5 minutes

	2 servings	*4 servings*	*6 servings*
French beans	**¼ lb** (113 grms)	**½ lb** (225 grms)	**1 lb** (450 grms)
Water	**1 tbl**	**2 tbls**	**3 tbls**
Salt	**a pinch**	**¼ teaspoon**	**½ teaspoon**
Black pepper	**¼ teaspoon**	**½ teaspoon**	**¾ teaspoon**
Butter	**a knob**	**a knob**	**a knob**

Place water in a shallow dish and stir salt in. Add beans, sprinkle them with black pepper and cover with pricked cling film. Cook on full power for 3 (4) (5) minutes. Pour off the liquid, dot with butter and cook again covered on full power for 30 seconds. Leave to stand covered for three minutes.

Variation of Vegetables à la grecque

CABBAGE

Preparation 5 minutes

	2 servings	*4 servings*	*6 servings*
Green cabbage or curly kale shredded	½ lb (225 grms)	1 lb (450 grms)	1½ lbs (725 grms)
Cooked potatoes	¾ lb (340 grms)	1½ lbs (725 grms)	2 lbs (900 grms)
Vegetable stock	1 tbl	2 tbls	3 tbls
Milk	¾ tbl	1¼ tbls	2 tbls
Butter	1 oz (28 grms)	2 oz (56 grms)	3 oz (85 grms)
Mace	shake	a pinch	¼ teaspoon
Salt and pepper to taste			

Place cabbage and stock in a bowl, cover with pricked cling film and cook for 5 (6) (8) minutes. Mash the potatoes with the milk and three-quarters of the butter. Mix the cabbage and potatoes with salt and pepper and mace to taste. Dot the rest of the butter on the mixture and reheat covered with pricked cling film.

SPICY CABBAGE

Preparation 5 minutes

	2 servings	*4 servings*	*6 servings*
Green cabbage shredded	½	1	1 large
Clove garlic crushed	½	1	1 large
Butter/margarine	½ oz (14 grms)	1 oz (28 grms)	1½ oz (42 grms)
Black peppercorns,	2	4	6
allspice berries and	2	4	6
juniper berries	4	8	12
crushed together			
Salt to taste			

Place some of the cabbage at the base of a large bowl, sprinkle with half the spices and add half the butter, continue in this way until all the ingredients have been used finishing with a little butter dotted over the cabbage. Cover with pricked cling film and cook on full power for 8 (10) (13) minutes. Leave to stand covered for 5 minutes.

WHITE CABBAGE   Renata Knobil

1 savoy cabbage
2 onions sliced
2 cooking apples thinly sliced
3 tbls brown vinegar

2 tbls sugar
A pinch nutmeg
Salt and pepper to taste

Place the cabbage leaves in a bowl with 6 tablespoons of water and cook on full power for 3 minutes, until it has come to the boil. Remove the cabbage, shred the leaves (not too finely) and reserve. Place 2 tablespoons of oil in a large bowl and add the onions and cooking apples and cook them on full power for 3 minutes. Stir in the cabbage and rest of ingredients and sauté them for another 3 minutes, until cooked but not mushy.

SWEET AND SOUR RED CABBAGE   Patricia Julius

Preparation 5 minutes   **Advance**

	2 servings	*4 servings*	*6 servings*
Red cabbage trimmed and shredded	½ lb (225 grms)	1 lb (450 grms)	1½ lbs (675 grms)
Onion finely chopped	1 small	1 medium	1 large
Cooking apple chopped	1 small	1 large	1½ large
Margarine/butter	1 tbl	2 tbls	3 tbls
Wine vinegar	1 tbl	2 tbls	3 tbls
Brown sugar	1 tbl	2 tbls	3 tbls
Salt	½ teaspoon	1 teaspoon	1½ teaspoons
Black pepper to taste			

Combine all the ingredients in a deep bowl until thoroughly mixed. Cover the dish with pricked cling film and cook on full power until cabbage is tender, 9 (11) (13) minutes, stirring occasionally during cooking. Leave to stand covered for 3 minutes, then drain off excess liquid, check the seasoning and serve hot.

BRAISED CELERY

Preparation 5 minutes

	2 servings	*4 servings*	*6 servings*
Celery strips	½ lb (225 grms)	¾ lb (340 grms)	1 lb (450 grms)
Onion sliced	1 small	1 medium	1 large
Butter/Margarine	½ oz (14 grms)	¾ oz (21 grms)	1 oz (28 grms)
Parve chicken stock	½ pint (284 ml)	¾ pint (426 ml)	1 pint (570 ml)
Salt and pepper to taste			

Melt margarine in a shallow dish by cooking on full power 30 (40) (50) seconds, add the strips of celery and onion, turn them over in the butter and cook on full power for 3 minutes. Add the stock and seasoning, cover with pricked cling film and cook on medium power for 8 (10) (15) minutes.

72

STUFFED PEPPERS

Preparation 10 minutes   Advance

	2 servings	*4 servings*	*6 servings*
Large green peppers	2	4	6
Filling			
Celery sticks	1	2	3
Onions finely chopped	1	2	3
Oil	1 tbl	2 tbls	3 tbls
Long grain rice	3 oz (85 grms)	5 oz (142 grms)	8 oz (225 grms)
Parsley chopped	1 tbl	2 tbls	3 tbls
Mixed herbs	shake	a pinch	¼ teaspoon
Salt	½ teaspoon	1 teaspoon	1½ teaspoons
Egg	1 small	1 medium	1 large
Black pepper to taste			
Sauce			
Margarine	1½ tbls	3 tbls	4½ tbls
Onion finely chopped	1 small	1 medium	1 large
Plain flour	2 teaspoons	1 tbl	1½ tbls
Tinned tomatoes chopped	6 oz (170 grms)	10 oz (283 grms)	15 oz (425 grms)
Chicken stock	¼ pint (142 ml)	½ pint (284 ml)	¾ pint (426 ml)
Tomato purée	1 teaspoon	2 teaspoons	3 teaspoons
Sugar	¼ teaspoon	½ teaspoon	¾ teaspoon
Salt	¼ teaspoon	½ teaspoon	1 teaspoon
Black pepper to taste			

Heat oil in dish on full power 2 (3) (3½) minutes, add onion and celery and cook on full power for 6 (7) (9) minutes until soft, stir in the rice, herbs and seasoning. Leave to cool for 5 minutes and then stir in the egg. Whilst they are cooking, cut off the tops of the peppers, and remove all the seeds. Stuff the peppers with the filling.

Sauce: Place the margarine in a bowl and cook on full power for 30 (40) (60) seconds, add the onion and cook for a further 3 (4) (5) minutes. Stir in the flour and gradually add the stock stirring all the time. Cook on full power for 2 (3) (5) minutes until it thickens and boils. Add the tomatoes, purée and seasonings. Stand the peppers in the sauce, cover with pricked cling film and cook on full power for 14 (18) (20) minutes until the peppers are cooked. Leave to stand for 5 minutes before serving.

PETITS POIS A LA FRANÇAISE   Sara Raiher

Preparation 10 minutes

	2 servings	4 servings	6 servings
Fresh shelled peas	1 lb (450 grms)	1½ lbs (675 grms)	2 lbs (900 grms)
Lettuce leaves shredded	1	2	3
Spring onions chopped	2	3	4
Water	1 tbl	1½–2 tbls	2 tbls
Sugar	½ teaspoon	1 teaspoon	2 teaspoons
Salt and freshly ground black pepper to taste			

Place the butter and spring onions in a shallow dish and microwave on full power for 1 minute, add the peas, water and pepper. Cover with the lettuce and pricked cling film and cook on full power for 3 minutes or until it comes to the boil. Cook for another 3 (4) (5) minutes on low power. Sprinkle with salt, stir and leave to stand covered for 2 minutes.

JACKET POTATOES

Preparation 5 minutes

Potatoes						
4 oz (113 grms)	1	2	3	4	5	6
Sour cream	½ tbl	1 tbl	1½ tbls	2 tbls	2½ tbls	3 tbls
Chives to sprinkle						
Butter						

Wash and dry the potatoes, prick well and wrap in kitchen paper. Place each potato in oven around the outside of the cooking dish with an inch (2.5 cm) between each one. Cook on full power for:

1 potato	5½ minutes	2 potatoes	6½–8 minutes
3 potatoes	10 minutes	4 potatoes	12 minutes
5 potatoes	16 minutes	6 potatoes	19 minutes

When cooked, leave covered to stand for 5 minutes. If desired cut potatoes in half and fill with either sour cream and chives or a knob of butter.

POTATOES A LA DINNY   Dinny Charkham

Preparation 10 minutes   **Freezable**

	2 servings	4 servings	6 servings
Potatoes thinly sliced	2 medium	4 medium	6 medium
Onion thinly sliced	¼ small	½ small	1 small
Button mushrooms sliced thinly	2	4	6
Tomatoes sliced thinly	1 small	1 medium	1 large
Oil	2 teaspoons	1 dessertspoon	1 tbls
Water	2 teaspoons	1 dessertspoon	1 tbls
Parsley chopped	¼ teaspoon	½ teaspoon	1 teaspoon
Salt and black pepper to taste			

Place the vegetables in layers in a suitable dish. Pour over oil and water and shake the dish. Sprinkle with salt and pepper and chopped parsley. Cover tightly with pricked cling film. Cook in microwave oven on full power for 3 (5) (8) minutes.

POTATO PUDDING
Gillian Burr

Preparation 10 minutes

	2 servings	*4 servings*	*6 servings*
New potatoes peeled and sliced thinly	½ lb (225 grms)	1 lb (450 grms)	1½ lbs (675 grms)
Cheddar cheese grated	1 oz (28 grms)	2 oz (56 grms)	3 oz (85 grms)
Parmesan cheese grated	2 tbls	4 tbls	6 tbls
Nutmeg	shake	a pinch	a teaspoon
Butter	½ oz (14 grms)	1 oz (28 grms)	1½ oz (42 grms)
Cream	2 tbls	¼ pint (142 ml)	7 fl oz (199 ml)
Salt and freshly ground pepper			

Pat the potato slices dry in a clean tea towel. Grease a casserole dish and place a layer of the potatoes on the bottom, season then pour some of the cream over the potatoes. Mix the two grated cheeses together. Sprinkle two tablespoons of the cheese over the cream. Dot with a little butter and continue layering the ingredients finishing with the cheese. Place a few dots of butter on the top, cover with pricked cling film and cook on full power for 10 (12) (14) minutes until the potatoes are soft. If desired this dish can be browned under a grill.

RATATOUILLE
Lynne Goldwyn

Preparation 15 minutes — Advance — Freezable

	2 servings	*4 servings*	*6 servings*
Courgettes thinly sliced	3 oz (85 grms)	5 oz (142 grms)	8 oz (225 grms)
Aubergines thinly sliced	¼ lb (113 grms)	½ lb (225 grms)	¾ lb (340 grms)
Green peppers finely chopped	2 oz (56 grms)	3½ oz (100 grms)	5 oz (142 grms)
Tomatoes skinned and chopped	3 oz (85 grms)	5 oz (142 grms)	8 oz (225 grms)
Parsley chopped	¾ tbl	1¼ tbls	2½ tbls
Sunflower oil	¾ tbl	1¼ tbls	2 tbls
Butter	¾ oz (21 grms)	1¼ oz (35 grms)	2 oz (56 grms)
Clove garlic crushed	½ large	1 small	1 large
Onion thinly sliced	1 small	1 medium	1 large
Black pepper to taste			
Salt	¾ teaspoon	1¼ teaspoons	2 teaspoons

Place butter and oil in a large dish and cook in a microwave oven on full power for 1 (1½) (2) minutes. Add onion and garlic, cook on full power for 3 (4) (5) minutes. Add the courgettes, aubergines, green pepper, tomatoes, parsley and salt. Turn the ingredients over in the fat. Cover the dish with pricked cling film. Cook on full power for 15 (18) (20) minutes. Cook uncovered for 3–6 minutes until most of the juice has evaporated. Check seasoning. Leave to stand for 5 minutes.

EASY SPINACH

Preparation 5 minutes

	2 servings	*4 servings*	*6 servings*
Fresh leaf spinach washed	¾ lb	1½ lbs	2 lbs
Butter	½ oz (14 grms)	1 oz (28 grms)	1½ oz (42 grms)
Nutmeg	shake	a pinch	¼ teaspoon
Salt and freshly ground pepper to taste			

Discard any thick stalks. Place the nutmeg, spinach and pepper in a pricked roasting bag leaving the open ends tucked underneath. Place on kitchen paper. Cook in a microwave oven on full power for 4 (5) (6) minutes. Stir in butter and salt and serve.

STUFFED TOMATOES

Preparation 5 minutes

6 large tomatoes

Stuffing

2 tbls sunflower oil or butter
2 onions chopped
5 oz (145 grms) **long grain rice**

1 teaspoon salt
¼ teaspoon black pepper
6 fl oz (170 ml) **boiling water**
1 oz (28 grms) **petits pois**
1 teaspoon oregano or basil

Cut tops from tomatoes and reserve. Remove flesh from tomatoes and chop. Drain the tomatoes and reserve. Melt margarine or oil in a casserole on full power for 1 minute, add onion and cook for further 2 minutes stirring once. Add chopped tomato flesh, rice, oregano or basil, salt and pepper and boiling water. Stir well and bring to the boil on full power 1–2 minutes. Cover with lid or pricked cling film and simmer on medium power for 5 minutes. Remove, add peas and cook on medium power for another 5 minutes or until the rice is tender. Stuff all the mixture into the tomatoes and cover with lid or pricked cling film. Cook for 5 minutes on medium power or reheat on full power when required.

PERFECT FLUFFY RICE
Caroline Young
Anchor Hocking MicroWare

Preparation 3 minutes   **Freezable**

	4 servings	*8 servings*
Long grain rice	8 oz (225 grms)	1 lb (450 grms)
Boiling water or stock	1 pint (570 ml)	1½ pints (860 ml)
Salt to taste if using water		
Micro Ware simmer cooker		

Place washed rice in casserole, pour over boiling liquid, stir once and cover with lid. Cook on full power for 13 (15) minutes. Let stand for 10 (12) minutes when it will complete its rehydration and become fluffy. Fork up before serving. If reheating from frozen, reheat in a freezer bag.

VEGETABLES A LA GRECQUE

Caroline Young
Anchor Hocking MicroWare

Serves 4–6   **Preparation 5 minutes**   **Cook 7 minutes**   **Chill 3 hours**

8 oz (225 grms) **button mushrooms**
8 oz (225 grms) **cauliflower broken**
   into tiny sprigs
2 tbls olive oil
1 clove garlic skinned and crushed
Salt and freshly ground
   black pepper to taste

¼ pint (142 ml) **dry white vermouth**
3 tbls tomato purée
2 tbls soft brown sugar
3 tbls marjoram or parsley
2 oz (56 grms) **onion thinly sliced**
2 tbls white wine vinegar
MicroWare supreme 2 litre casserole

In the casserole dish combine the oil, garlic and onion and cook on full power for 2 minutes. Stir in the vinegar, vermouth, tomato purée, sugar, herbs and seasoning. Add the vegetables coating well with marinade. Cover and cook on full power for 5 minutes, stirring once. Do not overcook, the vegetables should still be crisp. Cool, cover with the storage lid and place in a refrigerater until well chilled.

Variation: Omit vinegar, tomato purée, mushrooms and cauliflower. Substitute juice and finely grated zest of one large lemon, 8 oz (225 grms), young carrots cut into matchsticks and broad beans. Cook as above.

SALADS

WHOLE GREEN BEANS WITH FRESH TOMATO DRESSING

Serves 6   **Preparation 5 minutes**   **Cook 11 minutes**   **Chill 4 hours at least**

10 oz French beans cooked (280 grms)
4 oz onions thinly sliced (113 grms)
2 tbls oil
4 tbls water
1 clove garlic peeled and crushed
8 oz tomatoes peeled and chopped
  (225 grms)

2 tbls fresh mixed herbs chopped or
  1 tbl dried mixed herbs
3 tbls red wine vinegar
1 tbl soft brown sugar
Salt and ground black pepper to taste
MicroWare 16 oz main dish (450 grms)

Arrange beans in the dish, top with onions and water. Cover with lid and microwave on full power for 6 minutes. Partially remove lid to drain off water. Combine remaining ingredients in a bowl and cook on full power for 5 minutes. Pour evenly over the beans and onions. Cover with the lid and place in refrigerator until well chilled – preferably overnight.

CHICKEN AND BROWN RICE SALAD   Toshiba

Serves 4–6   **Preparation 5 minutes**   **Cook 30 minutes**

6 oz long grain brown rice (170 grms)
¼ cucumber diced
4 spring onions sliced
¼ green pepper chopped
¼ red pepper chopped
2 oz green olives (56 grms)
1 lb chicken cooked (450 grms)

Salad dressing
2 tbls sunflower oil
1 tbl lemon juice
1 teaspoon parsley
¼ teaspoon garlic salt
Salt and black pepper to taste

Place rice in a 4 pint (2.3 litre) bowl, cover with 1½ pints (850 ml) cold water and cook on full power for 30 minutes. Rinse in cold water and then mix in the salad ingredients.

Salad dressing: Combine all the ingredients and pour over the salad just before serving.

CORN AND ORANGE COLESLAW

Serves 6   **Preparation 10 minutes**   **Cook 1½ minutes**   **Advance**

9 oz white cabbage shredded (255 grms)
12 oz sweetcorn kernels with peppers
  (340 grms)
1 sweet apple cored and chopped
2 carrots grated
2 oz raisins (56 grms)
1 orange, flesh cut in pieces

Dressing
3 tbls crunchy peanut butter
¼ pint sour cream (142 ml)
2 tbls orange juice
Salt and black pepper to taste

Garnish: **Sprigs of watercress**

Drain the corn and reserve the juice. Mix the corn with the rest of the ingredients and place in serving bowl.

Dressing: Place all the ingredients including the reserved corn juice in a pyrex jug and cook on full power until hot but not boiling. Pour over the salad, toss well and garnish. Allow to cool.

CREOLE SALAD

Caroline Young
Anchor Hocking MicroWare

Serves 6   Preparation 3 mins.   Refrigeration 3 hours   Advance without garnish

Salad
8 oz cooked rice, still hot (225 grms)
10 oz tin sweet corn and peppers
  (280 grms)
3 tomatoes peeled and chopped
6 inch cucumber diced (15 cms)
4 oz smoked turkey in strips (113 grms)
Salt and black pepper to taste

Salad Dressing
1 tbl white wine vinegar
2 teaspoons Tabasco sauce
2 teaspoons coarse grain mustard
3 tbls olive oil
1 clove garlic, peeled and crushed
1 teaspoon soft brown sugar
Garnish: **Lettuce and strips of red pepper**

To cook rice see Vegetable section. Combine all the dressing ingredients in a screw-topped jar and shake well. Add the corn and peppers to the hot rice and stir in the dressing. Allow to cool. Blend in the tomatoes, cucumber and smoked turkey. Chill covered. Serve in lettuce leaf cups garnished with pepper strips. (Photograph on page 67.)

POTATO SALAD

Gillian Burr

Serves 6   Preparation 10 minutes   Cook 8 minutes   Advance

1 lb Jersey potatoes evenly sized
½ tbl walnuts broken into small pieces
1 tbl parsley chopped

¼ pint (142 ml) **vinaigrette dressing pre-prepared**
Salt and black pepper to taste

Scrub and cut the potatoes into small pieces and then place in a bowl, season, do not drain. Cover with pricked cling film and cook on full power for 8 minutes. Pour the dressing over and add the parsley and walnuts. Stir well and serve cold.

TABOULLAH

Miki Hildebrand

Serves 6–8   Preparation 5 minutes   Cook 10 minutes   Advance

Salad
8 oz cracked wheat (225 grms)
1 medium onion chopped
6 tbls parsley chopped
1 tbl fresh mint chopped
Boiling water
1 dessertspoon chives chopped

Salad Dressing
3 fl oz oil (85 ml)
3 fl oz wine vinegar (85 ml)
1 tbl water
½ teaspoon brown sugar
A pinch paprika
½ teaspoon soya sauce
½ teaspoon French mustard
Salt and black pepper to taste

Place the wheat in a bowl and pour over enough boiling water to cover, cook on full power for 7 minutes, then leave to stand for 10 minutes, drain and rinse well. Mix with the rest of the salad ingredients.

Salad Dressing: Combine all the ingredients and pour them over the salad. Mix well. Chill in refrigerator until required.

TUNA FISH AND PASTA SALAD
Gillian Burr

Serves 6   **Preparation 10 mins.**   **Cook 10 mins.**

½ lb pasta shells (225 grms)
8 French beans cooked
1 tin tuna fish in oil
5 radishes
1 tin corn kernels
2 tomatoes, firm
6 black olives
2 pints boiling water (1.14 litres)

Garnish: **Radish flower**

Salad Dressing
3 tbls sunflower oil
1 tbl wine vinegar
1 teaspoon lemon juice
½ teaspoon fresh chives chopped
½ teaspoon mustard powder
½ teaspoon sugar
Salt and black pepper to taste

Place the pasta shells in a large bowl and cover with the salted boiling water and cook on full power for 10 minutes. Rinse with cold water and drain well. Place the pasta in a shallow round fluted dish. Drain most of the oil from the tuna fish and flake it over the dish leaving a 1 inch (2.5 cm) border around the edge. Drain the corn and place a band of it around the edge of the dish. Place the radish flower in the centre of the dish, and then cut the tomatoes in half and then quarters and place them in a circle radiating from the radish. Use the beans to complete the sunburst design and fill up any gaps with slices of radish and the black olives.

Salad Dressing: Combine all the ingredients. Pour half over the salad an hour before it will be served and allow the pasta to absorb it. Pour the rest over just before serving.

TURMERIC RICE SALAD

Serves 6   **Preparation 5 minutes**   **Cook 30 minutes**   **Advance**

6 oz long grain brown rice (170 grms)
1¾ pints approx. boiling water (1 litre)
3 oz sultanas (85 grms)
1 garlic clove, crushed
½ teaspoon turmeric
Salt and black pepper to taste

Garnish
1 tbl chopped parsley

Salad Dressing
¼ pint sunflower oil (142 ml)
1 tbl cider
Juice from ½ lemon
1 teaspoon French mustard
½ teaspoon brown sugar
A pinch black pepper

Place the rice in a large bowl and cover well with boiling salted water and cook on full power for 30 minutes, leave to stand for 3 minutes and then rinse in cold water and drain. Add the rest of the ingredients.

Salad Dressing: Combine all the ingredients and pour them over the salad. Mix in well with a fork, adjust the seasoning and sprinkle with the chopped parsley just before serving.

SAUCES, STUFFINGS AND PRESERVES

SAUCES

Make the sauce in a larger jug or bowl than you think will be needed, as the mixture will expand considerably when cooked in a microwave oven. It will only be necessary to stir the sauce once or twice during the cooking time but the bowl must be large enough to allow you to whisk the sauce at the end of the cooking time.

Sauces may be prepared in the morning and will still taste and look as if freshly made when re-heated the same evening.

Reheat ½ pint (285 mil) of sauce on power 8 for 2 minutes covered with pricked cling film.

JAMS AND PRESERVES

Making jam is child's play in a microwave oven. It will not burn or stick. 2 lbs of fruit may be used at a time which should yield 4 lbs of jam. The only washing up incurred will be a large mixing bowl. The preserving jars may be sterilized in the microwave oven by half filling them with hot water and heating them on full power until the water boils. Then swirl the water around the inside of the jars, making certain you use an oven cloth to protect your hands, pour the water away and place the jars upside down on kitchen paper to drain.

SAVOURY SAUCES

APPLE SAUCE
Gillian Burr

Serves 6   **Preparation 5 minutes**   **Cook 8 minutes**   **Advance**   **Freezable**

1 lb cooking apples peeled
 and thinly sliced (½ kg)
2 tbls water
1 teaspoon lemon juice

½ oz margarine/butter (15 grms)
2 level teaspoons caster sugar
Salt and pepper to taste

Place apples in bowl and add the water. Cover dish with pricked cling film. Cook on full power for 8 minutes. Beat apples until smooth, add sugar, margarine or butter and seasoning to taste. Serve hot or cold with duck, goose, latkes, etc.

APRICOT POULTRY GLAZE

Makes 1 cup   **Preparation 2 minutes**   **Cook 2 minutes**   **Advance**

⅔ cup apricot jam
2 tbls orange liqueur

½ cup margarine
¼ teaspoon ground mace

Place margarine in pyrex jug and melt on full power – 30 seconds approximately. Stir in rest of ingredients. Cook on full power for 1½ minutes. Stir well and then brush on poultry. Cover with greased waxed paper which has been shaped like a tent.

BARBECUE SAUCE

Makes 12 fl oz (340 ml)   **Preparation 5 minutes**   **Cook 15 minutes**   **Advance**

8 oz onions chopped (225 grms)
2 oz sunflower oil (50 grms)
8 oz tomato purée (225 grms)
4 fl oz water (120 ml)
4 fl oz lemon juice (120 ml)

1 tbl Worcestershire sauce
¾ tbl prepared mustard
4 oz brown sugar (114 grms)
2 teaspoons salt
Black pepper to taste

Place all ingredients in large bowl and cook on full power for 4–5 minutes approximately, until boiling. Cook on full power for another 10 minutes.

BASIC BECHAMEL SAUCE

Makes ¾ pint (450 ml)   **Preparation 5 minutes**   **Cook 8 minutes**

¾ pint milk less 1 tbl if using cream (450 ml)
1 oz butter (28 grms)
1 oz plain flour (28 grms)
1 small onion thinly sliced
1 small carrot thinly sliced
1 stick of celery thinly chopped

1 clove of garlic chopped
4 white peppercorns
A pinch mace
1 bay leaf
1 tbl single cream (optional)
Salt and black pepper to taste

Place milk and vegetables with mace, bay leaf and peppercorns in a bowl and cook on full power for 4 minutes. In another bowl place the butter and cook on full power for 30 seconds until melted, stir in the flour and gradually add the strained milk mixture stirring constantly until smooth. Cook on full power for 2½–3 minutes. Then whisk with the cream (optional) until it thickens.

Variations

Capers – add 1 tbl
Horseradish – stir in 2 tbls of horseradish sauce
Mustard – add 1 tbl of prepared mustard
Anchovy – add 3–4 teaspoons of anchovy essence and 3 teaspoons of lemon juice
Mushroom – add ½ cup of mushrooms which have been lightly sautéed

CURRY SAUCE

Serves 4   Preparation 5 mins.   Cook 18 mins.   Standing time 10 mins.   Advance

1 oz margarine (28 grms)
1 large onion finely chopped
1 tbl curry powder
1 tbl plain flour

½ pint stock (275 ml)
2 tbls chutney
½ teaspoon garlic salt
A pinch cayenne pepper

Place onion with the margarine and cook on ¾ power for 6 minutes. Stir in the curry powder and flour until smooth and cook on the same power for another 2½ minutes. Stir in the stock until smooth and cook on full power for another 3 minutes. Add rest of the ingredients and cover with pricked cling film. Cook on full power for 7 minutes, stirring once or twice during that time. Check seasoning and allow to stand for 10 minutes before serving. Reheat when required.

FISH STOCK
Gloria Smith

Makes 2 pints (1.14 litres)   **Preparation 5 minutes**   **Cook 25 minutes**   **Freezable**

1 lb white fish bones (450 grms)   1 lemon rind
½ pint white wine (284 ml)   1 bay leaf
1 carrot sliced   6 peppercorns
1 onion sliced   2 pints cold water (1.14 litres)
2 oz mushrooms halved (56 grms)

Place bones in large bowl, add rest of the ingredients, cover lightly with pricked cling film. Cook for 10 minutes on full power. Skim. Cover again and cook on low power, No.3 for 15 minutes. Strain.

GRAVY

Serves 6–8   **Preparation 5 minutes**   **Cook 4 minutes**

2 tbls juice from roast beef   2 tbls cornflour
1 beef cube   Salt and pepper to taste
2 cups hot water or hot vegetable water

Pour the meat juices into a jug, stir in the crumbled stock cube and cornflour until it has become a smooth paste. Gradually stir in the hot water. Cook on full power for 3 minutes, until it comes to the boil, stirring 2–3 times during cooking. Season to taste and serve at once with the meat.

HOLLANDAISE SAUCE

Serves 3–4   **Preparation 2 minutes**   **Cook 2 minutes**

4 oz butter (114 grms)   Juice from 1 small lemon
2 egg yolks   Salt and pepper to taste
½ teaspoon dry mustard

Place butter in jug and cook on full power for 1 minute. Beat the egg yolks with the mustard, lemon juice and seasoning. Whisk this mixture into the hot butter for at least 25 seconds, then cook on medium power for another minute, whisking once during this time making certain that the sauce does not come to the boil. Whisk well to make the sauce smooth.

LEMON BUTTER
Jane Finestone

Serves 4   **Preparation 2 minutes**   **Cook 1½ minutes**   **Advance**   **Freezable**

4 oz butter (113 grms)   **Salt and pepper to taste**
1 tbl lemon juice

Cut butter into pieces and place in a bowl with the lemon juice and seasoning. Cook on full power for 1½ minutes. Stir well. Serve with vegetables.

PARSLEY SAUCE

Makes ¼ pint (150 ml)   **Preparation 5 minutes**   **Cook 4 minutes**   **Advance**

2 tbls parsley chopped   **2 tbls plain flour**
½ oz butter (15 grms)   **1 teaspoon lemon juice**
¼ pint milk (150 ml)   **Salt and freshly ground pepper to taste**

Place butter in a jug and cook on full power for 30 seconds until it has melted. Stir in the flour and then gradually stir in the milk and cook on full power for 2 minutes. Season to taste and whisk in parsley and lemon juice. Cook on full power for 1–1½ minutes until the sauce thickens. Whisk again. Delicious with fish dishes.

REDCURRANT POULTRY GLAZE

Makes ¾ cup   **Preparation 2 minutes**   **Cook 8 minutes**

½ cup redcurrant jelly   **2 tbls Crème de Cassis**
¼ teaspoon ground allspice

In a pyrex jug mix the ingredients. Cook in a microwave oven on full power for 1½ minutes approximately until the jelly melts, stirring twice during that time. Brush over the poultry and cover with greased waxed paper which has been shaped to form a tent.

SOYA POULTRY GLAZE

Makes ¾ cup   **Preparation 2 minutes**   **Cook 2½ minutes**   **Advance**

2 teaspoons cornflour   **⅔ cup water**
¼ cup soya sauce

Mix the cornflour and soya sauce to form a smooth paste, stir in the water and then cook on full power for 2½ minutes approximately until the sauce thickens, stirring several times whilst cooking. Brush the poultry with the glaze and cover with greased, waxed paper which has been shaped like a tent.

TOMATO SAUCE

Serves 6–8   **Preparation 5 minutes**   **Cook 8 minutes**   **Advance**   **Freezable**

2 oz butter/margarine (55 grms)
1 medium onion chopped
1 clove garlic crushed
14 oz tin peeled tomatoes (400 grams)

3 oz tomato purée (85 grms)
1 teaspoon dried mixed herbs
1 teaspoon caster sugar
Salt and black pepper to taste

Place butter, onion and garlic in bowl and cook on full power for 2 minutes. Add rest of ingredients and stir well. Cover with pricked cling film and cook on full power for 6 minutes stirring once after the first 3 minutes. Serve hot with pasta and cheese or purée and serve with meat balls or beefburgers.

SWEET SAUCES

APRICOT SAUCE

Serves 6   **Preparation 30 minutes**   **Cook 12 minutes**   **Advance**   **Freezable**

8 oz dried apricots (225 grms)
4½ oz sugar (126 grms)
8 fl oz water (225 ml)

1 inch cinnamon stick (2.5 cms)
Juice from 2 oranges

Soak the apricots in the water for at least 30 minutes. Add the cinnamon, cover with pricked cling film and cook on full power for 5 minutes. Leave to cool a little. Remove the cinnamon stick and then purée the apricots and the rest of the ingredients in a food processor or blender. Cook the mixture covered on full power for another 2 minutes. Serve hot or cold.

CARAMEL SAUCE

Gillian Burr

Serves 6	Preparation 5 minutes	Cook 17 minutes	Advance

1 cup granulated sugar
¼ cup cold water
½ cup hot water

1 teaspoon vanilla essence
2 teaspoons golden syrup
5½ oz tin condensed milk (140 grams)

Place sugar and cold water in pyrex bowl and cook on low power for 3 minutes. Stir well. Cook for a further 5 minutes, stirring well after the first two minutes. The syrup should have turned a light caramel colour. Allow to stand for 5 minutes then stir in the hot water. Stir in rest of ingredients. Cook on full power for 4 minutes, stir well after the first 2 minutes. Serve hot or cold.

CHOCOLATE SAUCE FOR ICE CREAM

Toshiba

Serves 4	Preparation 2 minutes	Cook 1 minute	Advance

2 oz plain chocolate broken up (56 grms) ½ oz butter (15 grms)
1 tbl milk

Place chocolate in bowl with butter. Heat on just under full power for 1 minute. Stir in the milk. This sauce may be reheated on low power if required.

CUSTARD

Serves 4–6	Preparation 5 minutes	Cook 5 minutes	Advance

2 rounded tbls custard powder
2 level tbls sugar

1 pint milk (550 ml)

Mix custard powder and sugar and stir in a little of the milk until it forms a smooth paste. Gradually stir in the rest of the milk. Cook on full power for 2 minutes, stir well and cook again until thickened – 2 minutes approximately. Serve hot or cold.

EGG CUSTARD SAUCE

Serves 4	Preparation 3 minutes	Cook 3½ minutes	Advance

2 egg yolks
1 cup milk

1 tbl sugar
½ teaspoon vanilla essence

Place eggs and milk in a bowl and beat together with a fork. Place the bowl in a Bain Marie containing 1 inch (2.5 cm) water, and cook on full power for 2 minutes, then stir. Cook for a further minute and then stir in the sugar and essence, cook for 1 minute. Should the mixture curdle quickly place it in a bowl of cold water and whisk it until smooth again. Serve hot or cold.

SUMMER FRUIT SAUCE

Lynne Goldwyn

Serves 6   Preparation 5 minutes   Cook 3 minutes   Advance   Freezable

8 oz combination of soft fruit (225 grms)   **2 oz caster sugar** (55 grms)

Place cleaned fruit and sugar in a bowl. Cover with pricked cling film and cook on full power for 3 minutes. Sieve. Check for sweetness. Serve hot or cold.

HOT FUDGE SAUCE

Serves 6–8   Preparation 2 minutes   Cook 3 minutes   Advance

3 oz brown sugar (85 grms)   **2 tbls milk**
2 level tbls cocoa powder sifted   **1 oz butter** (30 grms)
1 teaspoon vanilla essence

Place butter in bowl and cook on full power for 1 minute until butter has melted. Stir in the rest of the ingredients and cook on full power for 2 minutes. Stir. Serve hot or cold.

LEMON SAUCE

Serves 4   Preparation 5 minutes   Cook 6 minutes

Rind and juice from 1 lemon   **2 egg yolks**
A pinch cornflour   **Water**
2 oz caster sugar (56 grms)

Place lemon juice in pyrex jug and add water to make up to ¼ pint (140 ml). Stir in the cornflour and lemon rind until smooth. Cook on full power for 2 minutes. Stir again. Then stir in the sugar with the egg yolks. Cook on full power for 4 minutes, stirring once during that time. The sauce should have thickened and be served hot.

MOCHA SAUCE

Serves 6   Preparation 5 minutes   Cook 4 minutes   Advance

2 oz demerara sugar (56 grms)   **2 teaspoons strong black coffee**
½ oz butter (15 grms)   **3 tbls water**
4 oz plain chocolate chopped (113 grms)

Place sugar, water and coffee in a pyrex jug and cook on full power until the mixture boils – 2½ minutes approximately. Add the butter and chocolate and stir it until the chocolate has melted and the sauce has become smooth.

PEACH SAUCE
Lynne Goldwyn

Serves 4   **Preparation 5 minutes**   **Cook 3 minutes**   **Advance**   **Freezable**

4 ripe peaches skinned   **2 teaspoons maraschino**
2 tbls rum   **2 teaspoons caster sugar**

Place peaches in blender or food processor and purée. Sieve and place in bowl. Stir in other ingredients. Cover with pricked cling film and cook on full power for 3 minutes. Serve hot or cold.

RASPBERRY SAUCE

Serves 4–6   **Preparation 5 minutes**   **Cook 7 minutes**   **Advance**   **Freezable**

8 oz frozen raspberries (225 grms)   **1 tbl lemon juice**
3 tbls sugar

Place ingredients in a bowl and stir. Cover with pricked cling film and cook on full power for 7 minutes. Sieve. Serve hot or cold.

WALNUT BUTTER SCOTCH
Anne Moss

Makes ¼ pint (150   ml)   **Serves 3–4**   **Preparation 5 minutes**   **Cook 3 minutes**
2 tbls golden syrup   **5 tbls cold water**
2 tbls brown sugar   **5 tbls cold milk**
¾ oz butter (20 grms)   **½ oz walnuts chopped finely** (15 grms)
1 tbl cornflour/custard powder   **½ teaspoon lemon juice**

Place the golden syrup, brown sugar and butter in a pint (600 ml) glass measuring jug or bowl. Cook in a microwave oven on full power for 30 seconds. Open the door, stir to complete melting the chocolate and then cook on full power for 30–45 seconds or until the mixture bubbles. Blend the cornflour or custard powder, water and milk together and mix into the syrup. Cook on full power for 1½–2 minutes or until boiling, stirring once or twice during cooking. Stir in the walnuts and lemon juice. Serve hot with ice cream or baked apples.

STUFFINGS

FISH STUFFING

Preparation 10 minutes

	Serves 6	Serves 10
Fish	3 lbs (1.36 kg)	5 lbs (2.26 kg)
Butter	2 tbls	¼ cup
Onion chopped	¼ cup	½ cup
Celery chopped	½ cup	1 cup
Carrot	¼ cup	½ cup
Apple chopped	¼ cup	½ cup
Toasted sunflower kernels	1 tbl	2 tbls
Plain yoghurt	¼ cup	½ cup
Cooked brown rice	½ cup	1 cup
Salt and pepper to taste		

Place the vegetables with the butter in a large bowl and cook on full power for 4–6 minutes until the vegetables are cooked. Stir in the nuts, rice and apple and fold in the yoghurt. Season. Stuff the whole fish with the ingredients.

NUT STUFFING FOR DUCK   Toshiba

Preparation 10 minutes

¼ egg beaten
1 stick celery chopped
1 oz mixed nuts chopped (28 grms)

1 generous sprig fresh rosemary
2 teaspoons orange marmalade
4 level tbls white breadcrumbs

Mix together and use to stuff either a whole duck basting with some extra marmalade for the last few minutes of cooking time, or use to stuff individual breast portions, and again glaze with a little extra marmalade for the last few minutes of cooking time.

ORANGE RICE STUFFING

Preparation 5 minutes   Cook 3–6 minutes

	Serves 2	Serves 4	Serves 6
Butter/margarine	2 tbls	4 tbls	6 tbls
Celery chopped	2 tbls	4 tbls	6 tbls
Onion chopped	2 tbls	4 tbls	6 tbls
Pine nuts/pecans chopped	2 tbls	4 tbls	6 tbls
Raisins	2 teaspoons	1 tbl	1½ tbls
Orange juice	2 tbls	4 tbls	6 tbls
Osem parve chicken bouillon cube	½	1	1½
Chopped orange flesh	⅓ cup	⅔ cup	1 cup
Orange peel finely grated	¼ teaspoon	½ teaspoon	¾ teaspoon
Cooked rice	⅓ cup	⅔ cup	1 cup
Salt and pepper to taste			

This recipe is cooked on full power throughout. Place butter and vegetables and nuts in a bowl. Cook for 2 (3) (4) minutes. Mix the cube with the orange juice and stir it into the vegetables. Cook for 1–2 minutes, stir to ensure that the cube has dissolved. Add the orange peel and flesh and the rice, season and use to stuff chicken or duck.

SWEET PRESERVES

LEMON CURD

Makes 2 lbs (900 grms)   Preparation 5 minutes   Cook 12 minutes

1 lb caster sugar (450 grms)   ¼ lb butter (100 grms)
4 eggs   4 pint casserole dish (2.2 litres)
Juice from 3 lemons   Warmed jars
Grated rind from 1 lemon

The lemons will yield more juice and zest if heated in a microwave oven on full power for 1 minute before squeezing. Put sugar, butter, juice and rind of lemon into the container and cook for 8 minutes on full power stirring frequently. During this time the sugar should dissolve and come to the boil. Add the well beaten eggs, and return to the microwave oven, cook on full power for 4 minutes stirring frequently until mixture thickens. Seal and label.

RHUBARB JAM

Makes 1½ lbs (675 grms)   Preparation 5 minutes   Cook 30 minutes

1 lb rhubarb washed and cut into 1 inch   1 lb sugar (450 grms)
  (3 cm) pieces (450 grms)   4 pint casserole dish (2.2 litres)
1 lemon   Warmed jars
1 orange

Place rhubarb in a large casserole. Cover and cook for 5–6 minutes. Meanwhile grate rind from lemon and orange. Squeeze and strain the juice from the lemon and the orange. Tie the pips in a scrap of cheesecloth. Add the rind, juice, pips and sugar to the cooked rhubarb. Stir well. Cook on full power for 20–25 minutes stirring regularly until thick and will gel on a cold plate. Remove pips. Seal and label.

STRAWBERRY JAM

Makes 2 lbs (900 grms)   Preparation 5 minutes   Cook 19 minutes

1 lb fresh strawberries prepared (450 grms)   1 lb caster sugar (450 grms)
1 fl oz lemon juice (28 ml)   Warmed jars

Cook fruit and lemon juice in the microwave oven on full power for 4 minutes, then beat to a pulp with a wooden spoon. Add sugar stirring well. Cook for 4 minutes on full power until sugar has dissolved and stir again. Cook for a further 11 minutes on full power, stirring once during cooking cycle and again at the end of the cooking cycle. Jam will set when left to cool. Seal and label.

SAVOURY PRESERVES

APPLE AND MINT JELLY

Makes 2½ lbs (1.13kg)   **Preparation 15 mins.**   **Cook 1 hour 15 mins.**   **Advance**

3 lbs green apples thickly sliced (1.35 kg)   Juice from 2 lemons
1 lb granulated sugar (450 grms) **per pint**   A few drops of green food colouring
   of juice (57 ml)   1 pint water (570 ml)
4 tbls fresh mint finely chopped   Warmed jars

Place apples, 1 tablespoon of mint and water in a large bowl. Cover with pricked cling film and cook on full power for 34 minutes stirring occasionally. Strain into a measuring jug and check the quantity of juice then pour it into a clean large bowl and cook on full power until boiling. Stir in the correct amount of sugar to the quantity of juice (see above), until dissolved. Cook on full power for 5 minutes. Add the mint and a few drops of food colouring. Cook again on full power for 20 minutes approximately, until setting point is reached. Allow to cool until a thin skin has formed on the top of the jelly, stir gently and spoon into the prepared jars. Seal and label.

SPICY CRANBERRY SAUCE

Makes 1¼ pints (0.65 litre) **Preparation 10 mins.** **Cook 30 mins. approx.** **Advance**

2 cups fresh cranberries   1 cup dried apricots cut into pieces
1¾ cups sugar   ¾ cup raisins
¼ cup vinegar   1 teaspoon orange rind grated
¼ cup Crême de Cassis   ½ teaspoon cinnamon
½ cup orange juice   ⅛ teaspoon ground cloves

Place sugar and orange juice in a large bowl. Cook on full power until boiling, stirring to dissolve the sugar – 6 minutes approximately. Stir in the rest of ingredients. Cover loosely with waxed paper and cook on full power for 5 minutes approximately – until boiling. Stir well. Cover again with the waxed paper and cook on low power for another 5 minutes stirring once or twice during that time. Remove the cover from the sauce and cook again on low power for 15 minutes approximately, until the mixture has become transparent, stirring it once or twice. Will keep for 1 month if refrigerated.

CUCUMBER RELISH

Makes 2 lbs (900 grms) **Preparation 2 hours Cook 9 mins. Cook month in advance**

2 large cucumbers diced   1 oz salt (30 grms)
2 onions chopped   ½ teaspoon celery seeds
½ pint vinegar (280 ml)   ½ teaspoon mustard seeds
3 oz granulated sugar (85 grms)   Warmed jars

Layer cucumber with onions and salt in a large bowl and leave to stand for 2 hours. Rinse well and allow to drain, meanwhile in a large bowl place the vinegar, sugar and seeds and cook on full power for 6 minutes stirring once or twice. Add the cucumber and onions and cook on full power for another 2 minutes. Stir and pour into the prepared jars.

SPICED ORANGES

Anne Moss

Makes 3–4 lbs (1.36–1.81 kgs)   **Preparation 5 minutes**   **Cook 40 minutes**

5 thin skinned oranges
½ pint white wine vinegar (284 ml)
12 oz granulated sugar (340 grms)

2 inch cinnamon stick (5 cms)
2 teaspoons whole cloves
Warmed jars

Wipe the oranges (do not peel) and slice into ¼ inch (½ cm) rings. Place in a large bowl with the water. Cover with pricked cling film and cook on full power until the rings are soft, 16–20 minutes. Drain the slices and discard the water. Place the vinegar, cloves, cinnamon and sugar in a large bowl and cook on full power for 10–12 minutes, stirring occasionally until the sugar has dissolved. Add the orange slices and cook covered on 30 per cent power until the peels are transparent, this will take 25–30 minutes. Using a slotted spoon, lift out the orange slices and pack into the warmed jars, adding a few cloves to each. Cook the remaining syrup on full power for 8–9 minutes and pour over the fruit. Seal and label. Serve with cold meats or duck.

REDCURRANT JELLY

Makes 2½ lbs (1.13 kg)   **Preparation 5 minutes**   **Cook 1 hour 5 minutes**   **Advance**

4 lbs redcurrants (1.8 kg)
1 lb granulated sugar for each pint of juice
   (455 grms)
½ pint water (280 ml)

Jelly bag
Clean warm jars
Seals and labels

Place redcurrants and water in a large bowl and cook on full power for 15 minutes. Strain through the jelly bag without squeezing it to prevent the jelly being cloudy. Pour the juice into a measuring jug then return to a large bowl and cook on full power for 4 minutes. Stir in the correct quantity of sugar per amount of juice and continue cooking on full power for 45 minutes, stirring several times in the first 5 minutes to ensure that the sugar has dissolved before it comes to the boil. After that stir every 8–10 minutes. When setting point has been reached pour the jelly into the prepared jars. Seal and label.

DESSERTS FOR MEAT MEALS

When a recipe calls for dried fruit, instead of soaking the fruit overnight in water just wash the fruit, place it in a large bowl, cover with water and cook on full power for 7 minutes, then leave to stand for 5 minutes.

If you wish to remove the skins from peaches, heat whole peaches in the oven on full power for 20–30 seconds, stand for 10 minutes and then slide the skins off.

To stew cooking apples: just slice the apples into a glass bowl, sprinkle each layer with sugar and pour over a little water, cover with pricked cling film and cook on full power for 8 minutes.

FLAN PASTRY
Pat Fine

5 oz (142 grms) **butter**   **8 oz** (225 grms)**flour**
2–3 oz (56–85 grms)

Line flan ring with cling film. Place butter in Pyrex bowl and microwave until melted. Stir in sugar until well amalgamated. Add flour. Stir well. Butter a 10 inch (25.4 cms) flan ring and spread pastry with a wooden spoon or with your hand. Prick pastry well. Microwave on full power for 5 minutes. If pastry rises just press down again. Remove from dish when cold, brush with jam and fill with whipped cream. Decorate.

RICH SHORTCRUST PASTRY FLAN CASE
Anna Larking

6 oz (170 grms) **plain flour**   **2 tbls caster sugar**
3 oz (85 grms) **butter or margarine**   **1 egg yolk**
2 tbls water   **Pinch of salt**

Mix the egg yolk and sugar. Add water and stir. Sift the flour and salt and rub in the fat. Add the egg mixture and mix well. Knead together lightly and chill for 30 minutes, then roll out into a circle 2″ (5 cm) larger than the dish. Carefully line your flan dish, easing the pastry in gently. Cut the excess pastry away but do leave a little extra to allow for shrinkage during cooking. Line the case with greaseproof paper or kitchen paper. Cook on full power for 4–4½ minutes. Remove the paper lining and cook on full power again for a further 1–2 minutes. Allow to cool before filling.

FRENCH APPLE TART
Anna Larking

1 × 8″ (20.3 cms) **rich pastry flan case**   **2½ oz** (70 grms) **caster sugar**
 (see above)   **1 tbl apricot jam**
1½ lbs (675 grms) **cooking apples peeled** **1 tbl lemon juice**
1 oz (28 grms) **margarine**

Melt the butter on full power for 20 seconds,then add the apples (except one of them) and the sugar. Cover and cook on full power for 8 minutes, stir, then leave to cool. Slice the remaining apple thinly and sprinkle with lemon juice. Cover with pricked cling film and cook on full power until transparent – about 2 minutes. Leave to cool. Heat the apricot jam until liquid – about 30 seconds. Meanwhile, spread the apple purée into the base of the pastry case, arrange the apple slices on top of the purée so that they overlap each other. Glaze with apricot jam. If serving with a milk meal offer with whipped cream.

DRIED FRUIT COMPOTE   Bernice Burr

Serves 6   **Preparation 5 minutes**   **Cook 12 minutes**   **Advance**

½ **lb pears** (225 grms)   1 **orange chopped**
½ **lb apricots** (225 grms)   3 **strips angelica/green citron peel**
½ **lb prunes** (225 grms)   2 **tbls brandy**
1 **lemon chopped**   ¼ **cup honey**

Place the dried fruit in a bowl and cover with enough water to cover the fruit, and cook on full power until soft, 7–8 minutes approximately. Place chopped lemon and orange pieces in another bowl, cover with water and honey and cook on full power until soft. Mix all the fruit together. Reduce the fruit juices until they become a syrup, pour over fruit and add the brandy. Decorate with angelica or green citron peel. Serve cold.

CHOCOLATE FUDGE PUDDING   Ann Harris

Serves 4–5   **Preparation 10 minutes**   **Cook 5 minutes**   **Advance**

3 **oz self raising flour** (85 grms)   *Sauce*
2 **tbls cocoa**   4 **oz brown sugar** (113 grms)
4 **oz margarine** (113 grms)   2 **tbls cocoa**
4 **oz caster sugar** (113 grms)   ½ **pint water** (284 ml)
2 **eggs**
2 **tbls boiling water**

Heat all the sauce ingredients on full power for 2–3 minutes until they are really hot, stirring once or twice to dissolve the sugar. Place the pudding ingredients in a food processor and blend for 1 minute, then pour into a microwave cake dish and cover with the sauce. Cook the pudding on full power for 5 minutes and leave to stand for 4 minutes delicious for a family meal.

CARAMEL ORANGES   Jane Finestone

Preparation 5 mins.	**Cook 12 mins.**	**Chill 4 hours**	**Freezable 2 months**
	2 servings	*4 servings*	*6 servings*
Oranges peeled	2	4	6
Caster sugar	3 oz (85 grms)	6 oz (170 grms)	9 oz (255 grms)
Water	3½ tbls	7 tbls	10½ tbls
Orange liqueur	½ tbl	1 tbl	2 tbls

Cut oranges into slices and arrange in a serving dish or reshape oranges on cocktail sticks. Sprinkle them with liqueur. Place the sugar and water in a separate bowl and cook on full power for 9–12 minutes or until golden brown. Pour over oranges and chill.

DELICIOUS PEACH DESSERT Susie Barnett

Preparation 5 minutes   **Cook 1 minute**   **Advance**   **Freezable**

	2 servings	*4 servings*	*6 servings*
Peaches peeled	2	4	6
Pure orange juice	1 tbl	2 tbls	¼ pint (142 ml)
Orange squeezed	½ orange	1 small orange	1 large orange
Liqueur or white wine	2 tbls	3 tbls	5 tbls

Place the juice from the squeezed orange with the pure orange juice and some sugar in a jug and cook in a microwave oven on full power for 45 (50) (60) seconds. Pour the juice over the peaches, which have been sliced into a bowl, and leave to become cold. Stir in the liqueur or white wine. Place in a refrigerator until chilled.

SPICED PEACHES

Serves 6   **Preparation 2 minutes**   **Cook 8 minutes**   **Advance**   **Freezable**

2 x 15 oz tins peach halves (426 grms)	**½ teaspoon ground cinnamon**
6 cloves	**½ teaspoon ground nutmeg**

Place peaches or apricots with their juice in a bowl and add the rest of the ingredients. Cover with pricked cling film and cook on full power for 8 minutes. Leave in syrup until required.

BRANDIED PEARS WITH CHOCOLATE Jilly Barget

Preparation 8–12 minutes   **Advance (for pears)**

	2 servings	*4 servings*	*6 servings*
Pears peeled, halved and cored	2	4	6
Lemon rind	a pinch	½ teaspoon	¾ teaspoon
Water	¼ pint (142 ml)	½ pint (284 ml)	¾ pint (426 ml)
Brandy	2½ fl oz (70 ml)	¼ pint (142 ml)	7 fl oz (200 ml)
Sugar	2 oz (56 grms)	4 oz (113 grms)	6 oz (170 grms)
Cinnamon	shake	a pinch	¼ teaspoon
Chocolate	2 oz (56 grms)	4 oz (113 grms)	6 oz (170 grms)
Butter/Margarine	a dot	a knob	a large knob
Flaked almonds toasted	½ oz (14 grms)	1 oz (28 grms)	1½ oz (42 grms)

Place pears, water, brandy, sugar, cinnamon and a little lemon rind in a large bowl. Cover with pricked cling film and cook on full power for 5 (6) (7) minutes. Drain the pears and reserve the juice. Break the chocolate into small pieces and place with the butter/margarine in a small dish, melt on full power for 2 minutes approximately, stirring once during that time. Stir in 3 (6) (9) tablespoons of the juice. Pour chocolate over pears and decorate with toasted flaked almonds.

SPICED PEARS IN WINE

Lynne Goldwyn

Preparation 5 minutes **Cook 8–12 minutes** **Freezable 2 months**

	2 servings	*4 servings*	*6 servings*
Firm pears evenly shaped	**2**	**4**	**6**
Red wine	**¼ pint** (142 ml)	**½ pint** (284 ml)	**¾ pint** (426 ml)
Water	**¼ pint** (142 ml)	**½ pint** (284 ml)	**¾ pint** (426 ml)
Caster sugar	**1 oz** (28 grms)	**2 oz** (56 grms)	**3 oz** (85 grms)
Cinnamon stick	**1 inch** (2.5 cms)	**2 inch** (5 cms)	**3 inch** (7.5 cms)
Cloves	**2**	**4**	**6**
Ground nutmeg	**shake**	**a pinch**	**¼ teaspoon**
Lemon peel strips	**1 small**	**1**	**2**
Lemon juice	**¼ teaspoon**	**½ teaspoon**	**¾ teaspoon**
Flaked almonds	**1 tbl**	**2 tbls**	**3 tbls**

This recipe is cooked on full power throughout. Peel the pears but leave on the stalks. Place the rest of the ingredients except the almonds in a bowl, cover with pricked cling film and cook for 4 (5) (6) minutes. Stand pears in the liquid and cook for another 4 (5) (6) minutes. Leave to stand for 5 minutes then remove the cinnamon stick and lemon peel. Sprinkle the pears with the flaked almonds and serve.

DESSERTS FOR MILK MEALS

HINTS

The microwave oven cooks many dishes very easily that on a conventional hob would require a lot of attention and stirring to prevent burning and sticking. An example of this is making caramel for cream caramels or brûlées.

You require 4 fl oz (114 ml) water and 6 oz (170 grms) caster sugar. They should be placed in a large glass bowl and cooked without stirring on full power for 10–12 minutes, until a bubbling caramel has formed. Remove from the oven using oven gloves to protect your hands and stir in 2 tablespoons of hot water, return the mixture to the oven and heat on full power for 30 seconds.

Lemons and Oranges   Many recipes require lemon or orange peel or their juices; a microwave oven makes both tasks easier.
Place the fruit in the microwave oven and cook on full power for 15–20 seconds, the peel will be softer and thus easier to grate and the fruit will yield considerably more juice than it would have done.

Ice Cream When you wish to turn ice cream out of a mould, place it in the microwave oven and heat on defrost power for 25–30 seconds.

CHOCOLATE MOUSSE   Elizabeth Futler

Serves 10

2 bars Terry's Dark Bitter Chocolate   **8 soupspoons caster sugar**
7 eggs   **8 oz** (225 grms) **butter**

Melt chocolate and butter together in the microwave. Separate eggs. Whisk the sugar into the yolks, then whisk in the chocolate mixture. Beat egg whites in a bowl and then fold them into the chocolate mixture.

POTS DE CHOCOLAT WITH PRALINE   Patricia Julius

Serves 4–6   Preparation 10 minutes   Cook 3 minutes   Chill 1 hour   Advance

6 oz plain chocolate (170 grms)   **1 teaspoon brandy**
4 tbls strong coffee cold   **6 fl oz double cream** (170 ml)
1 oz butter (28 grms)   **3 oz praline crushed** (85 grms)
1 tbl caster sugar   **1 tbl chocolate grated**

Place the chocolate in a bowl and cook in a microwave oven on full power for 3 minutes until the chocolate has melted. Beat thoroughly, then add the butter, sugar, brandy and praline. Leave to cool slightly, whip the cream and fold most of it into the chocolate mixture, reserving the rest for decoration. Divide the mixture between four to six small dishes, depending on their size, and chill for at least 1 hour. Decorate with the remaining cream and a little grated chocolate.

CHOCOLATE SHORTBREAD   Susan Schottlander

Makes 48 fingers Preparation 5 minutes Cook 4 minutes Refrigerate 2 hours Advance

1 lb (450 grms) **plain chocolate**
  digestive biscuits crushed   **2 dessertspoons caster sugar**
8 oz (225 grms) **unsalted butter** **2 tbls golden syrup**
8 oz (225 grms) **drinking chocolate** **12½×9½ inch** (32×24 cms) **Swiss roll tin**

Place the butter in a jug and cook on full power for about 2 minutes until melted. Add the sugar, golden syrup and chocolate powder. Cook on full power for 2 minutes, stirring once. Pour on top of the digestive biscuits, mix well and then spread evenly in a shallow tin. Leave for at least 2 hours in the refrigerator. Cut the shortbread into biscuits and serve with whipped cream.

CLAFOUTIS PERIGORD
Elissa Bennett

Serves 8   Preparation 15 minutes + 5 hrs fruit soaking time   Cook 8 minutes

Fruit filling
2 oz (56 grms) **raisins**
¼ pint (142 ml) **boiling water**
8 oz (225 grms) **pitted prunes halved**
4 tbls brandy
1 oz (28 grms) **butter**
10 inch (25.4 cms) **round dish**
　　1½ inch (3.8 cms) **deep approx.**

Egg mixture
3½ oz (100 grms) **caster sugar**
4 large eggs
2 oz (56 grms) **plain flour**
Pinch salt
½ pint (284 ml) **milk**
½ teaspoon vanilla essence

Place the raisins in a bowl with the boiling water and leave for 10 minutes, then drain them. Then place the raisins in a jar with the prunes and add the brandy. Replace the lid and leave them for 5 hours minimum stirring them occasionally. Grease the cooking dish using all the butter.

Whisk the sugar, eggs and salt in a large mixing bowl, sift in the flour gradually, whisking it continuously. Stir in the milk and the contents of the jar. Ladle the mixture into the dish and cook on full power until its sides are well risen and the centre just set. Serve warm and freshly made.

PEACH DESSERT
Ruth Lipton

Serves 6   Preparation 10 minutes   Cook 15 minutes   Freezable

Cake
6 oz self raising flour (170 grms)
4 oz caster sugar (113 grms)
3 oz butter (85 grms)
1 egg
4 tbls cold milk

Topping
4–6 peaches fresh or tinned
1½ oz butter (42 grms)
2 tbls flour
4 oz soft brown sugar (113 grms)
Dish 11 inch x 7 inch (28 cms x 18 cms)

Cake: Place all the cake ingredients in a bowl and beat until smooth. Peel the peaches and slice half of them into ⅛ inch slices and place with the cake mixture in the dish. Cut the rest of the peaches in half and place on top of the cake mixture.

Topping: Melt the butter in a bowl on full power for 30 seconds, mix in the rest of the ingredients and sprinkle on top of the peaches. Cook on full power for 5–6 minutes.

COLD STRAWBERRY SOUFFLE
Lesley Levy

Serves 6   Preparation 5 mins.   Cook 30 seconds   Standing time 2 hours   Advance

½ pint strawberry purée (284 ml)
1½ tbls lemon juice
2 tbls white wine
4 tbls water

2 tbls powdered kosher gelatine
4 oz caster sugar (113 grms)
½ pint double cream (284 ml)
6 egg whites stiffly whipped

Place wine, water and gelatine in jug, mix together thoroughly and cook on full power for 30 seconds. Stir to ensure gelatine has dissolved. Add strawberry purée, lemon juice and sugar and stir thoroughly. Allow to cool, stirring once or twice. Whip the cream stiffly and fold in, then whip the whites and gently fold them into the mixture. Spoon the mixture into a soufflé dish or individual ramekin dishes. Place in a refrigerator until set.

SNACKS AND SUPPER DISHES

HINTS

Many of the dishes included in this section could be used as a starter, or a main meal. In the same way many of the dishes in the starter section may be useful when looking for supper dishes.

Eggs cook very quickly in a microwave oven and it is a good idea to remove them just before they appear cooked as they will continue to cook after being removed from the oven.

Most dishes freeze well, so when making a dish it is a good idea to make double quantity and freeze half. Reheating frozen food in a microwave oven is very quick and easy.

When cooking long pasta such as spaghetti lay it in an oblong dish, well covered with boiling water, add a teaspoon of salt and a tablespoon of oil. Halfway through the cooking time give the pasta a quick stir, then cover for the rest of the time. Leave to stand for 5 minutes before draining.

AUBERGINE PARMIGIANI   Renata Knobil

Serves 6–8   Preparation 10 minutes   Cook 12 minutes   Advance   Freezable

3 aubergines
1 clove garlic crushed
1 x 14 oz tin tomatoes (397 grms)
1 small onion chopped
4½ oz tomato purée (128 grms)
3 teaspoons parve chicken broth powder

1 teaspoon dried parsley
1 teaspoon oregano
1 lb Mozzarella cheese, or substitute
  grated (450 grms)
Salt and pepper to taste
¼ pint milk (142 ml)

Slice the aubergines with the skin on and dip them in milk. Lightly fry in oil until golden brown, then drain on absorbent paper. Transfer the oil to a large casserole and add the garlic, onion, tomato purée, tomatoes, chicken broth powder, parsley and spices. Cook on medium power for 6 minutes, stir the sauce and check that the tomatoes are not lumpy – if they are, continue to cook on low power for another 5 minutes. Place a layer of aubergines in a dish and cover it with a generous helping of the tomato sauce and lots of grated cheese, repeat with another layer of each. Cook on full power until the mixture is hot and the cheese has melted.
N.B. If preferred the aubergines may be sautéed in the microwave oven for 5 minutes on full power before draining on the paper.

CANNELLONI

Serves 4   Preparation 10 minutes   Cook 25 minutes

8 green cannelloni tubes
Filling
2 teaspoons tomato purée
4 oz onions finely sliced (113 grms)
1 clove garlic crushed
½ teaspoon dried basil
½ teaspoon dried oregano
7 oz tin tuna in oil (198 grms)
Salt and pepper to taste

Sauce
1 pint white sauce cooked (568 ml)
4 oz mushrooms sliced (113 grms)
2 oz Cheddar cheese grated (56 grms)
1 teaspoon lemon juice
Garnish
1 tbl Parmesan cheese grated
2 tbls parsley chopped

Filling: Place the onion, garlic and herbs in a bowl, cover with pricked cling film and cook on full power for 5 minutes. Add the tomato purée, salt and pepper, stir well and cook on full power for 3 minutes. Flake the drained tuna fish and stir into mixture, then cover again and cook on full power for another 3 minutes. Set aside. Add the mushrooms, cheese, and lemon juice to the white sauce and reserve. Using a teaspoon, fill the tubes with the filling and place side by side in a shallow casserole dish, pour over the sauce and cover with pricked cling film. Cook on full power for 14 minutes. Leave to stand for 3 minutes. Garnish and serve hot.

CHEESE FONDUE

Ruth Arnold

Serves 4–6   **Preparation 5 minutes**   **Cook 6–8 minutes**

1 garlic clove peeled and halved
1 lb Swiss cheese shredded (450 grms)
¼ cup plain flour
2 cups dry white wine
¼ teaspoon nutmeg

2 tbls Kirsch (optional)
Salt and pepper to taste
French bread cut into 1 inch (2.5 cms) cubes
1½ quart casserole (1.70 litres)

Rub the inside and bottom of the casserole with garlic. Combine cheese, flour, salt and nutmeg in the prepared casserole dish, add wine and mix well. Cover with pricked cling film and cook on full power for 6–8 minutes, stirring occasionally until the cheese has melted, stir in the Kirsch. Spear squares of French bread with fondue forks and dip in fondue.

CHEESE AND VEGETABLE PUDDING

Miki Hildebrand

Serves 4–6   **Preparation 10 minutes**   **Cook 14 minutes**

Base
2 oz butter (56 grms)
1 oz Gruyère cheese grated (28 grms)
1 medium onion chopped
4 oz cauliflower florets (113 grms)
8 oz broccoli frozen and defrosted (225 grms)
1 oz ground almonds (28 grms)
4 tbls dry white wine
Salt and pepper to taste
3½ pint soufflé dish (2 litre)

Topping
½ pint milk (284 ml)
2 oz butter (56 grms)
2 oz plain flour (56 grms)
1 tbl wholegrain mustard
5 oz Gruyère cheese grated (142 grms)
¼ teaspoon ground nutmeg
4 eggs separated

Garnish: Sour cream

Grease the inside of the dish with the butter and then cover thickly with the grated cheese. Shake out the excess. Place the vegetables in another bowl, cover with pricked cling film and cook on full power for 3 minutes. Place the cooked vegetables in the soufflé dish and smooth the top. Add the wine, salt and pepper and sprinkle the almonds over them.

Topping: Pour the milk into a large jug and heat on full power for 3 minutes. Place the butter in a bowl and cook on full power for 1 minute until melted, then stir in the flour and mix throroughly. Gradually stir in the hot milk, whisking it until the sauce is smooth. Cook on full power for 1½ minutes, whisk again and then cook for a further minute. Whisk in the egg yolks, mustard, salt and pepper and then the cheese. Whisk the egg whites until stiff and the fold into the rest of the topping. Pour the mixture over the vegetables and sprinkle the nutmeg on top. Cook on full power for 7 minutes, then serve immediately garnished with a little sour cream.

CHEESY LEEKS

Preparation 5 minutes

	2 servings	4 servings	6 servings
Leeks small	½ lb (225 grms)	1 lb (450 grms)	1½ lbs (675 grms)
Parmesan cheese grated	2 teaspoons	1 tbl	1½ tbls
Butter	½ oz (14 grms)	1 oz (28 grms)	1½ oz (42 grms)
Lemon juice	½ tbl	1 tbl	1½ tbls
Salt	¼ teaspoon	½ teaspoon	¾ teaspoon
Freshly ground black pepper to taste			

Cut the white part of the leeks into 1 inch (2.5 cm) pieces. Melt the butter in a shallow dish on full power for 30 (40) (50) seconds and add the leeks and salt. Cover with pricked cling film and cook on full power for 6 (7) (9) minutes. Add the lemon juice and cook for another 1–3 minutes until the leeks are tender. Cover with the cheese and sprinkle with black pepper and leave covered to stand for 2–3 minutes. The cheese may be browned under a hot grill if desired.

COURGETTE CASSEROLE
Rosanna Burr

Preparation 10 minutes

	2 servings	4 servings	6 servings
Courgettes sliced	½ lb (225 grms)	1 lb (450 grms)	1½ lbs (675 grms)
Onion chopped	1 small	1 medium	1 large
Cheddar cheese	1 oz (28 grms)	2 oz (56 grms)	3 oz (85 grms)
Butter	2 oz (56 grms)	3 oz (85 grms)	4 oz (113 grms)
Tabasco sauce	2 drops	4 drops	6 drops
Soft breadcrumbs	1 oz (28 grms)	2 oz (56 grms)	3 oz (85 grms)
Salt	¼ teaspoon	½ teaspoon	¾ teaspoon
Eggs beaten, size 3	1	2	3
Black pepper to taste			

Place the courgettes in a sieve and sprinkle with salt, leave to drain for 10 minutes and then pat dry. Meanwhile, melt two-thirds of the butter in a casserole dish on full power 30 (50) (60) seconds and add onion and cook on full power for 2 (3) (4) minutes until they are soft. Add the courgettes, cheese, Tabasco sauce, beaten eggs and salt and pepper and mix well. On your hob, fry the breadcrumbs in the last third of the butter until golden brown and then sprinkle on the courgette mixture. Cover with pricked cling film and cook on full power for 5 (6) (7) minutes until the courgettes are soft.

EGGS ELISSIA

Elissia Noble

Serves 2–4   **Preparation 5 minutes**   **Cook 12 minutes**

A knob butter
1 onion chopped
½ red pepper chopped
½ green pepper chopped

1 potato thinly sliced
4 eggs
4 tbls milk
Salt and black pepper to taste

Place all the vegetables in a medium sized casserole and place the butter on top. Cover loosely with lid and cook on full power for 7 minutes. Beat together the eggs, milk, salt and pepper and pour the mixture around the edge of the dish over the vegetables. Replace the lid and cook for a further 3–5 minutes. Stir half way through this time. Slide onto a plate and serve with green salad.

SCRAMBLED EGGS

Serves 1   **Preparation 3 minutes**   **Cook 1 minute**

1 teaspoon butter
2 large eggs
Hot buttered toast

Salt and pepper to taste
2 tbls milk

Place butter in a bowl and cook on full power for 20–30 seconds until it has melted. Add the eggs, milk, salt and pepper and beat with a fork. Cook on full power for 40 seconds, stirring half way through that time. Place on top of the buttered toast and serve immediately.

WELSH RAREBIT

Serves 4   **Preparation 5 minutes**   **Cook 5 minutes**

1 tbl butter or margarine
1 tbl plain flour
8 oz Cheddar cheese grated (225 grms)
A pinch cayenne pepper
A pinch mustard powder
A pinch salt

4 tbls beer
4 drops Worcestershire sauce
4 egg yolks
4 slices toasted bread

Garnish: **Parsley sprigs**

Place butter in a bowl and melt on full power for about 30 seconds, stir in the flour and cook for another minute. Stir in the cheese, salt, mustard, cayenne pepper, beer, Worcestershire sauce and the egg yolks. Cook on full power until the mixture thickens – 2–3 minutes. Butter the toast then place the cheese mixture on top. Place under a hot grill until brown, 1–2 minutes. Serve immediately, garnished with the parsley and grilled tomatoes if desired.

HADDOCK CASSEROLE   Gloria Smith

Serves 4   **Preparation 10 minutes**   **Cook 15 minutes**

4 haddock steaks skinned
4 tomatoes quartered
¼ pint (142 ml) milk
Salt and freshly ground black
   pepper to taste

1 large onion sliced
¼ lb (113 grms) mushrooms sliced
A knob butter
3 oz (85 grms) Cheddar cheese grated

Place the haddock in a casserole. Cover with a layer of onions, tomatoes and mushrooms. Add salt and pepper. Pour the milk over, dot with butter. Cover loosely with pricked cling film and cook on full power for 9–12 minutes depending on thickness of fish. Sprinkle grated cheese over the top, dot with butter and brown under a hot grill until the cheese is bubbling.

MACKEREL ROLLS WITH RHUBARB SAUCE   Gloria Smith

Serves 4   **Preparation 15 minutes**   **Cook 15 minutes**

4 large mackerel filleted
2 bay leaves
½ teaspoon salt
5 fl oz (142 ml) dry cider
1 teaspoon black peppercorns
A knob butter

Sauce
8 oz (225 grms) rhubarb chopped
A squeeze lemon juice
A pinch nutmeg
2 tbls dry cider
2 tbls soft brown sugar
Garnish
Lemon wedges

Roll mackerel fillets and keep together with cocktail sticks. Place in shallow casserole and pour the cider over them. Add bay leaves and peppercorns, salt and dot with butter. Cover loosely with pricked cling film and cook on full power for 10–12 minutes. Remove the fish from the liquid and keep warm.

Sauce: Place rhubarb, cider, lemon juice, sugar and nutmeg in a bowl and cook uncovered for 3–4 minutes on full power. Stir until it is puréed. Place each fillet at the side of a dish and place some of the sauce by the fish. Garnish with lemon wedges.

N.B. Herrings may be substituted for the mackerel.

MUSHROOM AND RICE PILAFF

Preparation 10 minutes

	2 servings	4 servings	6 servings
Long grain rice	4 oz (113 grms)	6 oz (170 grms)	8 oz (225 grms)
Button mushrooms sliced	4 oz (113 grms)	6 oz (170 grms)	8 oz (225 grms)
Onion sliced	½	1 small	1
Clove garlic	¼	½	1
Celery sticks chopped	1	1 large	2
Red pepper deseeded and chopped	½	1 small	1
Green pepper deseeded and chopped	½	1 small	1
Cashew nuts	1 oz (28 grms)	2 oz (56 grms)	3 oz (85 grms)
Boiling salted water	½ pint (285 ml)	¾ pint (425 ml)	1 pint (568 ml)
Olive oil	¾ tbl	1¼ tbls	2 tbls

Place oil, garlic and onion in a bowl and cook on full power for 3 (4) (5) minutes, stir in the rice, celery and peppers and cook them on full power for 1 (1½) (2) minutes. Add the water and cook for another 3 (4) (5) minutes, stir in the mushrooms and cook for a further 5 minutes, stirring in the nuts after the first 3 minutes. Leave to stand, covered, for 7–8 minutes before serving.

PIPERADE

Preparation 10 minutes

	2 servings	4 servings	6 servings
Oil	1 tbl	2 tbls	3 tbls
Onion finely chopped	1 medium	1 large	2 medium
Red pepper sliced	½	1	1½
Green pepper sliced	½	1	1½
Tomatoes peeled and quartered	2	4	6
Eggs	2	4	6
Salt and pepper to taste			

Heat oil in large bowl on full power for 1½ minutes and stir in onion and garlic. Cover with pricked cling film and cook on full power for 3 (3½) (4½) minutes. Stir in the peppers and cook for a further 2 (3) (4) minutes. Season and add the tomatoes to the onion mixture, cover again and cook on full power until the vegetables are soft 3 (4) (5) minutes. Beat the eggs and pour over the vegetables, stir gently and cook until barely set, stirring once or twice during cooking.

SPINACH AND CHEESE PANCAKES Judy Jackson

Makes 8 pancakes   **Preparation 15 mins.**   **Cook 15 mins. apart from pancakes**
Freezable

Pancakes
4 oz (113 grms) **plain flour**
2 teaspoons salt
2 eggs
8 fl oz (227 ml) **milk**
2 teaspoons oil
Extra oil for frying

Filling and sauce
1 lb (450 grms) **fresh spinach**
1 oz (28 grms) **butter**
1 oz (28 grms) **flour**
½ pint (284 ml) **milk**
Salt and pepper to taste
Topping
¼ lb (113 grms) **grated Cheddar cheese**

Pancakes: Make pancake batter by mixing the first 4 ingredients together, adding the milk gradually to make a smooth batter. Leave to stand for 15 minutes. Make the pancakes by swirling a little oil round a small frying pan and pouring back any excess. Heat and pour in just enough batter to make one pancake and cook over high heat for a few minutes. With a palette knife carefully turn it over and cook on the other side. Continue until the batter is used up, stacking the pancakes between sheets of greaseproof paper. At this stage the pancakes may be frozen or refrigerated until needed.

Filling: Wash the spinach well and place in a deep dish, season well. Do not add any liquid. Microwave on full power for 4–7 minutes until cooked. Drain and chop the cooked spinach.

Béchamel Sauce: Melt the butter on full power for about 30 seconds, add the flour and stir well. Heat the milk slightly in the oven and then gradually stir it into the flour and butter mixture. Cook on full power for about 7 minutes, stirring every minute until all the milk has been absorbed and the sauce has become smooth and thick. Add the chopped spinach and seasoning to taste.

To assemble the pancakes: Divide the filling between the pancakes and spread it down the centre of each one. Roll up and arrange the filled pancakes in a serving dish, fairly close together. Sprinkle with grated cheese. To reheat: cover the dish and reheat on full power for about 3 minutes. Test to see if they are hot – the cheese will have melted and the filling should be hot. If you prefer, flash under a hot grill to brown the cheese and crisp the edges.

TUNA STUFFED PANCAKES

Serves 4   **Preparation 10 minutes**   **Cook 8 minutes**

8 cooked pancakes
7 oz (198 grms) **tinned tuna in oil**
1 tbl grated onion
½ pint (284 ml) **hot white sauce**
1 teaspoon prepared mustard
Salt and pepper to taste

Topping
2 tbls lemon juice
5 fl oz (142 ml) **sour cream**
2 tbls fresh chives chopped

Stir the drained, flaked tuna, onion, mustard, salt and pepper into the white sauce and then spread equal amounts of it over the pancakes. Roll them up and place them side by side in a dish. Sprinkle with lemon juice and cover with pricked cling film and cook on full power for 8 minutes. Pour the soured cream over the pancakes and sprinkle the chives over the cream. Serve immediately.

TIJUANA CHILLI PASTA

Serves 8   Preparation 10 minutes   Cook 45 minutes   Advance

Freezable without pasta

2 lbs (900 grms) minced beef
8 oz (225 grms) onion chopped
½ pint (284 ml) beef stock
2 × 14 oz (397 grms) tins of tomatoes
2 tbls tomato purée
2 oz (56 grms) plain flour

2 teaspoons mild chilli powder
½ teaspoon black pepper
1 teaspoon oregano
8 oz (225 grms) mushrooms sliced
1 teaspoon salt
8 oz (225 grms) pasta spirals cooked

Place the meat and onion in a casserole and cook on full power for 8 minutes, stirring occasionally. Drain any excess liquid. Stir in the flour, tomatoes, tomato purée, the spices, herbs and seasoning with the stock. Cover with a lid or pricked cling film and cook on full power for 20 minutes, stirring the mixture occasionally. Check for seasoning then add the cooked pasta and cook on full power until hot.

STUFFED TOMATOES   Jackie Miller

Serves 2   Preparation 5 minutes   Cook 8 minutes

2 beefsteak tomatoes
2 fl oz (56 ml) double cream
1 oz (28 grms) butter
1 egg
2 oz (56 grms) mushrooms chopped

2 oz (56 grms) onion chopped
Salt and black pepper to taste
Garnish optional
1 tbl breadcrumbs
½ tbl Parmesan cheese

Cut tops off tomatoes and scoop out the flesh (you may use it for another dish). Place tomatoes on kitchen paper to drain. Mix the double cream and egg together. Season to taste. Place the mushrooms, onions and butter in the oven and cook on full power for 2 minutes until soft, stirring once. Mix the cream mixture into the mushrooms and onion, and spoon into the tomatoes. Cook on medium power for another 4 minutes.

Garnish: Mix the cheese with the breadcrumbs and sprinkle on top of the tomatoes. Place under a hot grill for 2 minutes until brown.

BISCUITS, BREADS,
PETITS FOURS AND DRINKS

BISCUITS

CHOCOLATE BISCUITS
Jane Finestone

Makes 12   **Preparation 5 minutes**   **Cook 6½ minutes**   **Advance**

2 oz wholemeal flour (56 grms)
2 oz self raising flour (56 grms)
4 oz porridge oats (113 grms)
1 oz dark brown sugar (28 grms)

½ teaspoon baking powder
4 oz butter softened (113 grms)
4 tbls milk
Covering
12 oz plain chocolate (340 grms)

Combine all ingredients except chocolate. Mix thoroughly and knead to a soft dough. Roll onto a floured board to ¼ inch (6.35 millimetres) thick and cut into 2 inch (5 cms) rounds. Place biscuits on a tray in the oven and cook on full power for 3½ minutes. They are cooked when they can be removed from the tray without breaking easily. Cool on a wire tray. Melt the chocolate on full power for 3 minutes approximately, stirring after each minute. Coat the biscuits with the chocolate. Harden the biscuits on a wire tray or non-stick parchment paper.

COCOA CRACKLE BISCUITS

Makes 16   **Preparation 5 minutes**   **Cook 1½ minutes**   **Advance**

3 oz butter (85 grms)
2 tbls golden syrup
3 level tbls cocoa powder sifted

3 oz cornflakes (85 grms)
3 level tbls caster sugar
16 paper cases

Place butter and syrup in a large bowl and cook on full power for 1½ minutes. Stir in the sugar and cocoa powder. Gently, using a large metal spoon, fold in the cornflakes until they are evenly coated with the syrup. Spoon the mixture into the cases and refrigerate until cold.

TEATIME FLAPJACKS
Gloria Smith

Makes 9   **Preparation 5 minutes**   **Cook 3½ minutes**   **Advance**

3 oz soft dark brown sugar (85 grms)
3½ oz butter (100 grms)

2½ oz porridge oats (71 grms)
2 oz jumbo oats (56 grms)

Melt butter and sugar in a small square dish (MicroWare versatility pan) on full power for 30 seconds. Mix all ingredients together into the dish and flatten down neatly. Cook on full power for 3 minutes. Leave until cold, then turn out and cut into portions.

EAT ME BISCUITS   Miki Hildebrand

Makes 45 approx.   **Preparation 5 minutes**   **Cook 3½ minutes each batch**

½ cup butter
1 cup rolled oats
1 cup plain flour
1 cup sugar
1 cup dessicated coconut

1 tbl golden syrup
1 teaspoon bicarbonate of soda
2 tbls boiling water
Glass turntable of oven or flat round dish
   which has been greased

Mix the coconut, sugar, flour and rolled oats in a large bowl and reserve. Place the butter, and golden syrup in a small bowl and melt on full power for 2 minutes approx. Add the soda which has been mixed with the boiling water, stirring the liquid into the centre of the dry ingredients and mixing with a wooden spoon until the mixture is fairly stiff. Drop teaspoons of the mixture around the edges of the dish leaving about 1½ inches (3.8 cms) between them. Cook on full power for 3–3½ minutes until they are golden brown in the centre. Leave on the dish for a few minutes until you are able to lift them onto a wire tray to cool. Repeat until all the mixture has been used.

LEMON SHORTBREAD

Makes 8 wedges   **Preparation 5 minutes**   **Cook 4 minutes**   **Advance**

2½ oz brown sugar (71 grms)
4 oz butter (113 grms)
5 oz plain flour (142 grms)
3 tbls ground rice
½ teaspoon baking powder

½ teaspoon salt

Topping
Rind from ½ lemon, grated
1 tbls light brown soft sugar
7 inch (18 cms) fluted flan dish

Cream the butter and sugar until light and fluffy. Sift the flour, ground rice, salt and baking powder together and mix well with the butter and sugar to form a dough. Line the dish with cling film and press the dough into it, smoothing the top. Mark into 8 even wedges. Sprinkle the lemon rind and sugar over the top and gradually press in. Cook on full power for 3–4 minutes. Allow to cool slightly, then cut into wedges and turn out onto a wire rack to cool completely. Store in an airtight tin.

PEANUT CRUNCHIES   A Peanut Lover

Makes 25 approx.   **Preparation 5 minutes**   **Cook 2½ minutes each batch**

1¼ cups self raising flour
½ cup butter
⅔ cup brown sugar
½ teaspoon cinnamon

1 tbl coffee essence
⅓ cup roasted peanuts
Greased oven turntable or flat round dish

Sieve the flour and cinnamon into a Kenwood bowl then add the rest of the ingredients and beat to form a stiff dough. Drop 8 rounded teaspoons of the mixture around the edges of the dish as evenly spaced as possible. Cook on full power for 2 minutes approx. until the biscuits are golden brown, allow to cool until just firm, then remove carefully onto a wire tray. When completely cold, store the biscuits in an airtight tin.

MERINGUES
Sheilagh Goodman

Makes 24   **Preparation 2 minutes**   **Cook 1½ minutes each batch of 8**

1 egg white   **12 oz icing sugar** (340 grms)

Mix the two ingredients into a paste. Divide the mixture into 24 small balls and place 8 at a time on Bakewell paper. Cook them on full power for 1½ minutes. Repeat with the rest of the mixture. Store in an airtight container.

BREADS

HINTS

To refresh stale bread: Place the bread in a paper bag covered with a tea towel. Heat until the cloth feels just warm, when the bread will be ready to serve. If the bread is very stale wrap it in wet kitchen paper. Do eat it within 20 minutes of freshening.

To thaw frozen bread: Stand the slices of bread on kitchen paper. Heat on defrost power.

BROWN ROLLS

Makes 16   **Preparation 15 minutes**   **Prove 30 minutes**   **Cook 3½ minutes**

12 oz wholemeal flour (340 grms)
4 oz plain flour (113 grms)
1 teaspoon salt
2 teaspoons dried yeast
1 teaspoon sugar
½ pint milk (284 ml)

2 teaspoons malt extract
2 tbls vegetable oil
Garnish
Beaten egg to glaze
Sesame or poppy seeds
**Round flat tray lined with
    parchment paper**

Place the milk in a jug and cook on full power for 30 seconds until just hot. Stir in the yeast and sugar and leave in a warm place until frothy, 10–15 minutes. Sift the flours and salt into a bowl and cook on full power for 30 seconds, make a well in the centre and stir in the yeast mixture, 1 tablespoon of the oil and the malt extract. Work the dough until it leaves the sides of the bowl clean. Turn onto a floured board and knead it until it is smooth and no longer sticky. Add a little more tepid milk if it is too dry. Oil the bowl a little and replace the dough, turn it over and then cover the bowl with cling film. Place the bowl in the oven and cook on full power for 5 seconds at a time every few minutes until the dough has doubled in size. Knead the dough on a floured board for 2 minutes, then divide into 16 pieces and form them into rolls. Brush with oil and leave half of them on the baking tray to rise for 20–30 minutes, until the dough springs back when lightly pressed with your fingertip. Cook the rolls on full power for 3–3½ minutes, turning them over after 2 minutes. Cook the rest of the rolls in the same way. While the rolls are still hot brush them with the beaten egg and sprinkle them with the seeds. Brown under a hot grill for 1–2 minutes.

QUICK BREAD

Makes 1 large loaf   Preparation 5 minutes   Cook 7 minutes   Brown 5 minutes

8 oz wholemeal flour (225 grms)
8 oz plain flour (225 grms)
2 tbls baking powder
1 teaspoon salt
2 oz butter (56 grms)

1 teaspoon vinegar
½ pint milk (284 ml)
2 tbls black treacle
Greased plate

Sift the flours and salt and baking powder together and place in a Kenwood bowl or food processor and rub in the butter until well mixed. Place the rest of the ingredients in a jug and cook on full power for 30 seconds. Pour the liquid into the centre of the flour and mix well, in a machine for 45 seconds–1 minute, or by hand for 2 minutes. Turn the dough onto a lightly floured board and knead for 2–3 minutes. Form into a 6 inch (15 cms) round and place on the greased plate. Mark the top with a deep cross using a floured knife to prevent it sticking and cook on full power for 6 minutes. Test with a skewer near the centre of the loaf; if it comes out clean the loaf is cooked, if not, cook on full power for another minute. Brown the loaf by putting it under a hot grill until all the sides are brown or place at the top of a very hot oven for 5 minutes to crispen the crust and improve its appearance.

QUICK CHEESE BREAD   Jane Finestone

Serves 6   Preparation 5 minutes   Cook 9 minutes

8 oz plain flour (225 grms)
2 teaspoons baking powder
2 teaspoons mustard powder
½ teaspoon salt

5 oz Cheddar cheese grated (142 grms)
2 oz butter (56 grms)
8 fl oz milk (227 ml)
2 eggs

This recipe is cooked on full power throughout. Mix flour, baking powder, mustard and salt, add 4 oz (113 grms) of the cheese. Place the butter in a bowl and cook for 1 minute until melted, stir in the milk and eggs mixing them until just blended. Add to the flour and beat until well mixed. Spoon into loaf dish and cook for 9 minutes. Sprinkle with remaining cheese. Cover with foil, but see that it does not actually touch the top of the bread. Leave to stand for 20 minutes and then turn the bread out. Nice with a salad lunch!

WHITE BREAD

Makes 1 lbs (450 grms) **loaf**   **Preparation 5 minutes**   **Cook and prove 1 hour**

1 lb plain flour (450 grms)
1½ teaspoons sugar
½ teaspoon salt
½ pint water (284 ml)

1 teaspoon active dried yeast
2 tbls vegetable oil
1 tbl butter
8½ inch loaf dish (22 cm)

Pour the water into a jug and heat on full power for 15 seconds. Mix in the sugar and yeast with a fork and leave in a warm place for 10–15 minutes until it becomes frothy. Sift the flour and salt into a large bowl and cook on full power for 30 seconds. Make a well in the centre and stir in the yeast mixture and the oil. Mix thoroughly until the mixture leaves the sides of the bowl and then turn out onto a floured board and knead for about 6 minutes, until the dough is really smooth. Oil the mixing bowl and replace the dough. Brush the top of it with oil and cover with cling film. Cook on full power for 5 seconds every few minutes until the dough has doubled in size. Place the butter in the loaf dish and cook on full power for 20 seconds until the butter has melted. Place the dough back on the floured surface and knead again for 2–3 minutes. Form the dough into the same length as the loaf dish but then turn it over so that it is covered with butter. Leave it to stand in the dish covered with cling film until it reaches practically to the top of the dish. Brush the dough with egg or milk and cook on low power for about 8 minutes until the bread is soft but resilient; then place it under a hot grill until it is golden brown, turning it over so that each side browns, or put it at the top of a very hot oven for 5 minutes to brown it.

Alternatively, cook in a conventional oven preheated to Gas No.8 – 450° (230°C) for about 30 minutes, until the loaf is golden brown and has shrunk slightly from the sides of the tin.

Brown Bread: Use the same recipe but substitute ½ lb (225 grms) wholemeal flour for ½ lb (225 grms) white flour.

TEA BREADS

DATE AND RAISIN LOAF
Gillian Burr

Makes 1 lb (450 grms) **loaf**   **Preparation 5 minutes**   **Cook 9 minutes**

3 oz raisins (85 grms)
3 oz dates chopped (85 grms)
1 teaspoon bicarbonate of soda
1 oz butter (28 grms)
6 oz plain flour (170 grms)
¼ pint orange juice (142 ml)

1 teaspoon baking powder
¼ teaspoon salt
3 oz soft brown sugar (85 grms)
½ teaspoon vanilla essence
1 large egg beaten
Loaf dish 9 inch x 4 inch (23 cms x 10 cms)

Sift the flour, salt and baking powder and reserve. Grease the loaf dish and line the dish with non-stick parchment. Place the orange juice in a mixing bowl and cook on full power until it is hot, 1–1½ minutes. Stir in the butter and bicarbonate of soda, then add the vanilla essence, raisins and sugar. Stir in the beaten egg, a little at a time. Fold in the flour mixture and the dates. Ladle the mixture into the loaf dish and cook on full power for 7–8 minutes until the top is just dry. The cake will continue to cook after it is removed from the oven. Lift out and place on a wire rack. Serve sliced and buttered the same day as cooked.

DATE AND WALNUT BREAD

Makes 1 lb (450 grms) **loaf**   **Preparation 5 minutes**   **Cook 5 minutes**

½ cup caster sugar
1 cup dates chopped
½ cup walnuts
1 large egg
1½ cups plain flour
¼ teaspoon vanilla essence
2 tbls margarine
**1 teaspoon bicarbonate of soda and ¾ cup
  boiling water blended together**

Decoration
Chopped walnuts
Chopped dates and glacé cherries

Lemon glacé icing
12 oz icing sugar (340 grms)
Juice from ½ lemon
A few drops yellow vegetable colouring
Tepid water

Grease a ring mould. Place all the ingredients in a Kenwood bowl and cream for 1½ minutes. Place the mixture in the prepared dish and spread evenly. Cook on full power for 4½ minutes – the top will still feel soft and slightly sticky, but will continue to cook after the cake has been removed from the oven. Allow the cake to remain in its dish on a wire cooling tray for a few minutes, and then turn out onto the wire tray until cold.

Icing: Sift the icing sugar into a bowl and gradually stir in the lemon juice and 2–3 drops of the yellow colouring. Add a little tepid water if required to make the icing smooth. Decorate with the fruit before the icing has completely set.

HONEY LOAF

Makes ¾ lb (340 grms) **loaf**   **Preparation 5 minutes**   **Cook 12 minutes**

12 oz plain flour (340 grms)
1 teaspoon baking powder
1 teaspoon bicarbonate of soda
½ teaspoon ground ginger
¼ teaspoon salt
½ teaspoon mixed spice

6 fl oz milk (170 ml)
6 tbls thin honey
2 tbls vegetable oil
1 egg
Loaf dish 7 inch x 4 inch (18 cms x 10 cms)

Sift all the dry ingredients together into a large bowl. Place the honey and milk in a jug and cook on full power for 30 seconds. Beat in the oil and egg. Pour onto the flour mixture and beat thoroughly. Ladle the mixture into the greased dish and cook on full power for 10–12 minutes, until the top is just dry. The loaf will continue to cook after it has come out of the oven. If you desire a browner finish place under a hot grill for a minute or place in the top of a hot oven for 3–4 minutes. Serve warm, buttered and sliced. If the bread is not used the same day, it is delicious toasted.

SWEETS AND PETITS FOURS

Sweets and Petits Fours are much quicker to make in a microwave oven and they do not boil over resulting in a mess to clear up. Another advantage is that it is not necessary to constantly stir the mixture as on a conventional hob. Making sweets is a wonderful holiday treat for children.

CHOCOLATE FUDGE   Gillian Burr

Makes 1 lb (450 grms)   **Preparation 5 mins.**   **Cook 10 mins. approx.**   **Advance**

12 oz caster sugar (340 grms)
1½ tbls golden syrup
¼ pint milk (142 ml)
1½ oz chocolate in pieces (42 grms)

1 oz butter (28 grms)
1 teaspoon vanilla essence
A pinch salt
Square 7 inch (17½ cms) **dish**

Place all the ingredients in a large bowl and cook on full power for 8–10 minutes, stirring frequently. The mixture should be tested to see if it has reached the 'soft ball' stage, which means that when a small amount is dropped in a glass of cold water it should form a soft ball. It is difficult to predict exactly how long this will take so it is advisable to test every minute after 7 minutes of cooking have taken place. Once the mixture has reached the 'soft ball' stage leave it to cool for 15 minutes and then beat it until it thickens and becomes dull in appearance. Spread evenly in the buttered dish and leave until nearly set, then cut into squares. Store in an airtight tin – provided it stays around long enough!

COCONUT ICE

Makes 27 balls or squares   **Preparation 5 mins.**   **Cook 4½ mins.**   **Advance**

¼ **pint sweetened condensed milk** (142 ml)   **Red and green food colouring**
8 oz dessicated coconut (225 grms)

Mix the milk and coconut together very well and then divide into 3 bowls. Add a few drops of green colouring to one, some red colouring to another and leave the third one plain. With damp hands form the contents of each bowl into nine balls or squares. Line the base of your oven with some kitchen roll, then place a third of the balls on it and cook on full power for 1½ minutes. Repeat until they are all cooked. Store in an airtight tin.

COFFEE FUDGE   Gillian Burr

Makes 1 lb (450 grms)   **Preparation 5 mins.**   **Cook 2 mins.**   **Advance**

3 oz butter (85 grms)   **1 tbl double cream**
1 lb icing sugar (450 grms)   **Square buttered 7 inch** (17½ cms)**dish**
3 bare tbls sweetened coffee essence

Place the butter and coffee essence in a deep bowl and cook on full power for 2 minutes. Gradually mix in the rest of the ingredients, then beat until smooth and creamy. Spread into the dish and leave until cool. Mark into squares. If desired some sultanas or a few walnuts, etc., may be added with the icing sugar.

ORANGE AND GINGER FUDGE   Anna Larking

Makes 24 squares approx.   **Preparation 5 minutes**   **Cook 12 minutes**   **Advance**

3 oz granulated sugar (85 grms)   **2 tbls orange juice**
¼ **pint evaporated milk** (142 ml)   **1½ oz stem ginger chopped** (42 grms)
1 orange rind grated   **Buttered tin 5 inch x 3½ inch**
                                      (12.7 cms x 8.9 cms)

Mix all the ingredients except the ginger in a large bowl and cook on full power for 12 minutes, stirring every 2 minutes. Add the ginger and beat with a wooden spoon until thick. Pour into the tin and leave to cool. When nearly set, mark into squares. Store in an airtight tin.

120

COCKTAIL PRUNES
Gillian Burr

Preparation 2 minutes   **Cook 5 minutes**   Advance

12 oz pitted dried prunes (340 grms)   **¾ cup sweet sherry or brandy**
½ lemon thinly sliced   **Jar with lid**

Place the ingredients in a bowl and cook on full power for 4 minutes then ladle them into a jar that they will completely fill. Cover and leave to cool then store in a cold place until required. The prunes should still be fairly firm.

CHOCOLATE ORANGE TRUFFLES

Makes 24   **Preparation 10 minutes**   **Cook 2 minutes**   Advance

12 oz icing sugar sifted (340 grms)   **1 egg yolk**
1½ tablespoons milk   **Grated peel from 1 small orange**
4 oz plain chocolate in pieces (113 grms)   **Dessicated coconut to garnish**
1 teaspoon vanilla essence   **Chocolate vermicelli to garnish**
1 oz butter (28 grms)   **Paper petits fours cases**

Place chocolate and butter in a bowl and cook on full power for 2 minutes. Stir in the sugar, vanilla, milk and egg yolk and thoroughly combine. Leave until cool and firm enough to roll into balls. Using damp hands roll some in coconut and some in the chocolate vermicelli. Place in paper petits fours cases.

FRUIT TRUFFLES
Anna Larking

Soaking time 2 hours   **Preparation 10 minutes**   **Cook 1½ minutes**   Advance

8 oz almond paste (225 grms)   **Icing sugar**
4 oz glacé cherries (113 grms)   **Greaseproof paper**
1 tbl brandy optional   **Paper cases**
4 oz plain chocolate (113 grms)

Soak the cherries in the brandy for at least 2 hours. Melt the chocolate on full power for 1½ minutes, stirring once during that time. Meanwhile, roll out the almond paste thinly and cut into 1½ inch–2 inch circles (4 cms–5 cms), depending on the size of the cherries. Wrap each cherry with a piece of almond paste, roll them in your hand until they are smooth and the shape of a ball. Using a cocktail stick, dip each ball into the melted chocolate. Place on greaseproof paper until set. Shake some icing sugar over them and place in the paper cases. Store in an airtight container.

RUM TRUFFLES
Anna Larking

Makes 16   **Preparation 5 minutes**   **Cook 1½ minutes**   **Advance**

4 oz plain chocolate (113 grms)   **2 oz icing sugar sieved** (56 grms)
2 tbls brandy   **2 oz ground almonds** (56 grms)
1½ oz butter unsalted (42 grms)   **Chocolate vermicelli**

Place chocolate and brandy in a bowl and cook for 1½ minutes on full power or until melted. Stir in the butter and then the icing sugar and almonds so that they are well blended. Leave in a cool place. When firm enough to handle divide into 16 even–sized pieces and roll into balls. Roll the balls in the chocolate vermicelli. Store in an airtight tin.

DRINKS

"BEDTIME CHOCOLATE DRINK" or

"THE REASON WHY WE BOUGHT THE MICROWAVE"
Chesterman children

2 heaped teaspoons drinking chocolate   **1 mug cold milk**

Place the drinking chocolate in a mug and fill with cold milk. Set the microwave for one minute on full power. Remove and stir briskly. Just right for a good night's sleep.

CAKES

HINTS

Cakes cooked in a microwave oven do not require cooking for long enough to become brown, therefore they look more appetising if they are made with coloured ingredients i.e. brown sugar as opposed to white.

When cakes are to be cooked in a microwave oven, the eggs should be beaten for as little time as possible.

To make plain cake more attractive, place a paper doyley on top of it and shake over some sifted icing sugar, stencilling the pattern on to the cake. Remove the doyley carefully.

Cakes rise to at least twice their original level so always use a deep dish – a much deeper one than that needed in a conventional oven.

Cakes continue to cook after they have come out of the oven so be careful not to overcook them or they will become tough.

CARROT CAKE

Preparation 10 minutes	Cook 8 minutes	Advance

7 oz (200 grams) **caster sugar**
6 fl oz (170 ml) **corn oil**
2 level teaspoons **ground cinnamon**
8 oz (225 grms) **carrots grated**
1 teaspoon **vanilla essence**
1 level teaspoon **baking powder**

Icing
6 oz (170 grms) **cream cheese**
Juice of 1 large lemon
4 level tbls icing sugar
Decoration
Pulp and juice of 2 passion fruit
9 inch (23 cm) **microwave ring dish**

Line the dish with strips of parchment paper so that you will be able to lift out the cooked cake. Beat the eggs, sugar, oil and vanilla essence in a large bowl. Sieve the flour, cinnamon and baking powder together and add to the mixture. Add the carrots and stir them until just mixed. Spoon the mixture into the cake ring and cover with parchment paper. Cook on full power for 8 minutes. Leave to stand for 5 minutes. Carefully lift the cake out using the parchment strips and allow to cool before icing.

Icing: Beat the ingredients together and, using a palette knife, spread the icing over the cake. Decorate with the pulp of the passion fruit and squeeze the juice on top.

CHEESECAKE   Deanna Kaye

Preparation 5 minutes	Cook 15 minutes	Advance	Freezable

Base
2 oz (56 grms) **butter**
4 oz (113 grms) **digestive biscuits crushed**

7 inch (18 cm) **disposable cake dish**
  lightly greased

Filling
2 oz (56 grms) **butter**
8 oz (225 grms) **cream cheese**
2 size 2 eggs separated
2 oz (56 grms) **caster sugar**
¼ pint (142 ml) **sour cream**
2 teaspoons **vanilla essence**

Base: Melt the butter for 1 minute on full power, then mix in the biscuits. Press into the base of the cake dish.

Filling: Cream butter and sugar, mix in the cream cheese, egg yolks, sour cream and vanilla essence. Whip the egg whites until stiff and fold into the mixture. Pour into the case and cook on defrost power for 14 minutes. Chill well before turning out carefully.

CHOCOLATE MOUSSE CAKE   Renata Knobil

Serves 8	Preparation 5 minutes	Cook 5 minutes	Advance	Freezable

6 eggs separated
7 oz **margarine** (200 grms)
7 oz **plain chocolate** (200 grms)
1½ teaspoons **liqueur or vanilla essence**

1 cup caster sugar
3 tbls self raising flour
Nuts to decorate

Melt margarine with chocolate and the liqueur or vanilla essence in a bowl on full power for 3–4 minutes, stirring every minute. Beat the egg yolks and add to the chocolate mixture. Beat the egg whites until stiff, then beat the sugar into them. Fold the whites into the chocolate mixture, then place ⅓ of it into a bowl and fold the flour into it. Place in a cake dish and cook on full power for 3–4 minutes until the top is just tacky (it will continue to cook for another 2 minutes after being removed from the oven). Place the mousse on top and freeze. Remove from freezer 15 minutes before serving and decorate with nuts.

CHOCOLATE LEMON CHEESECAKE   Anne Moss

Preparation 5 minutes   **Cook 17 minutes**   **Advance**   **Freezable**

Topping
2 oz (56 grms) **margarine**
2 oz (56 grms) **caster sugar**
8 oz (225 grms) **cream cheese**
Grated rind 1 lemon
2 tbls lemon juice
5 fl oz (142 ml) **sour cream**
2 eggs separated

Base
6 digestive biscuits
2 oz (56 grms) **butter melted**
2 oz (56 grms) **chocolate melted**
6 inch (15 cm) **soufflé or cake dish**
Decoration
Halved walnuts or fruit

Base: Mix the broken biscuits with the butter you have melted on full power for 40 seconds and press into the bottom of the cake dish. Melt the chocolate on full power for 2 minutes approximately, stirring after the first minute. Spread it over the biscuit base.

Topping: Cream the margarine and sugar together, add the cream cheese, the egg yolks, grated rind and juice and sour cream. Whip the egg whites until stiff and fold them into the cheese mixture. Pour onto the base and smooth the top. Cook on low power or power level 4 for 14 minutes. Leave to set overnight before turning out and decorating. Decorate with halved walnuts or fruit.

CHOCOLATE BROWNIES

Preparation 5 minutes   **Cook 5 minutes**   **Advance**

3 oz (85 grms) **butter/margarine**
4 oz (113 grms) **self raising flour**
4 tbls cocoa powder
4 oz (113 grms) **sugar**

2 tbls milk
2 eggs
1 teaspoon vanilla essence
2 oz (56 grms) **walnuts chopped**

Rectangular dish 5×8 inches (12.5×20 cms)

Place the butter and cocoa in a dish and cook on full power for 1½ minutes. Mix in the sugar. Beat together the eggs, milk and vanilla essence and then add the cocoa mixture. Stir in the nuts and flour, then cook on full power for 5 minutes. Leave to stand for 10 minutes. Allow to cool in the dish and then cut into squares.

CHOCOLATE CAKE

Deanna Kaye

Preparation 5 minutes   Cook 4 minutes   Advance

5 oz (142 grms) **plain flour**
1 oz (28 grms) **cocoa**
5 oz (142 grms) **soft dark brown sugar**
2 teaspoons **baking powder**

2 size 2 **eggs**
6 tbls **corn oil**
6 tbls **milk**
7 inch (18 cm) **greased plastic disposable cake dish**

Sieve the cocoa, baking powder and flour together and stir in the brown sugar. Mix the eggs, oil and milk together and add to the dry ingredients. Stir briskly. Pour the mixture into the container and cook on full power for 3½–4 minutes. The cake will be slightly tacky in the centre but will continue to cook when it is out of the oven.

CHOCOLATE REFRIGERATOR CAKE

Rosanna Burr

Preparation 10 minutes   Chill 6 hours minimum

Cake
8 oz (225 grms) **plain chocolate**
8 oz (225 grms) **unsalted butter**
2 **eggs beaten**
1 oz (28 grms) **caster sugar**
12 **plain biscuits broken up**
2 tbls **cognac**

2 oz (56 grms) **glacé cherries**
2 oz (56 grms) **walnuts chopped**

Decoration
5 fl oz (142 ml) **double cream whipped**
1 oz (28 grms) **chocolate coarsely grated**
1 lb (450 grms) **loaf dish**

This cake is cooked on full power throughout. Line the loaf dish with non-stick paper. Place butter and chocolate in a bowl. Cook for 2–3 minutes until melted, stirring once or twice. Add the eggs, sugar and cognac and beat well. Layer the chocolate mixture with layers of the fruit and nuts and the biscuits, finishing with a chocolate mixture layer. Refrigerate for several hours until the cake is firm. Lift, or turn out onto a plate. Decorate with swirls of the whipped cream and some coarsely grated chocolate.

CHOCOLATE RUM CAKE

Preparation 10 minutes   Cook 5–6 minutes

4 oz (113 grms) **soft margarine/butter**
4 oz (113 grms) **self raising flour**
8 oz (225 grms) **soft dark brown sugar**
½ teaspoon **bicarbonate of soda**
2 **eggs**
1½ oz (42 grms) **cocoa powder**
2 tbls **dark rum**
2 oz (56 grms) **ground almonds**
3½ fl oz (100 ml) **cold water**

Decoration
3 oz (85 grms) **plain chocolate grated**
½ pint (284 ml) **double cream whipped**
4 **black grapes halved and seeded**
4 **green grapes halved and seeded**
1 small **orange in segments**
7 inch (18 cm) **round cake dish greased**

Mix the cocoa and rum with the water and reserve. Sift together flour and bicarbonate of soda. Cream the margarine and sugar, gradually beat in the eggs, then stir in the cocoa mixture, sifted flour and ground almonds. Mix well and pour into the cake dish. Smooth the top and cook on full power for 5–6 minutes until the top is just cooked. Cool for 5 minutes and then turn out onto a wire rack until cold. Cut in half horizontally, and sandwich together with a third of the cream. Decorate the top and sides of the cake with the rest of the cream. Press the grated chocolate onto the sides of the cake and decorate the top with the fruit.

COFFEE CAKE
Sylvia Kursteiner

Preparation 10 minutes   **Cook 7 minutes**

4 oz (113 grms) **butter**
4 oz (113 grms) **soft dark brown sugar**
8 oz (225 grms) **self raising flour**
2 size 3 eggs beaten
5 tbls milk
1½ level tbls instant coffee powder
7½ inch (19 cm) **deep round cake dish**
  lined with cling film

Topping and Filling
½ pint (284 ml) **whipped cream**
2 teaspoons sifted icing sugar
2 teaspoons instant coffee powder
1 teaspoon dark rum

Decoration
10 whole hazelnuts

Blend flour, coffee, margarine and sugar. Stir in the eggs and milk to make a fairly soft batter. Spoon the batter into the dish and smooth the top. Cook on full power for 6½–7 minutes until the sides of the cake shrink slightly away from the dish. Leave to stand for 15 minutes and then turn out and leave until cold.

Topping: Mix the ingredients together.

To assemble the cake cut the cake in half horizontally. Spread the filling on one half and cover with the other half of the cake. Use the rest of the topping to cover the sides and top of the cake. Decorate with the hazelnuts.

FRUIT CAKE FOR SPECIAL OCCASIONS
Deanna Kaye

Preparation 15 minutes   **Cook 40 minutes**   **Stores for several weeks**

8 oz (225 grms) **butter**
6 oz (170 grms) **dark brown sugar**
4 beaten eggs
8 oz (225 grms) **plain flour**
Pinch of salt
1 teaspoon mixed spice
1 oz (28 grms) **ground almonds**
1½ oz (42 grms) **almonds chopped**
2 oz (56 grms) **candied peel finely chopped**
8 oz (225 grms) **currants**
6 oz (170 grms) **sultanas**
2 oz (56 grms) **stoned dates chopped**

Rind and juice 1 large orange
1 teaspoon rum
3 tbls brandy
1½ oz (42 grms) **walnuts chopped**
10 glacé cherries quartered
4 oz (113 grms) **raisins**

Decoration, optional
1 lb (450 grms) **almond paste**
1¼ lbs (565 grms) **royal icing**
8 inch (20 cm) **round cake dish greased**

Cream the butter and sugar together in a large bowl until light and fluffy, then beat the eggs in gradually and stir in the flour, salt and spices. Fold in gently the nuts, dried fruit, peel and orange rind and juice. Stir in the rum and brandy and pour into the cake dish. Cook on low power for 5 minutes, then draw the mixture from the sides into the middle of the dish with a fork. Cook on low power for another 15 minutes. Leave to stand for 15 minutes then cook again on low power for 15 minutes until the cake is just dry on top. Slide a knife around the edge of the cake and leave the cake in the dish to cool slightly before turning out onto a wire rack. When completely cold, wrap in foil, seal tightly and store in a cool place until a week before required.

Decoration: Cover the cake with almond paste and leave to dry for 3–4 days, then cover with the royal icing.

HONEY SPICED SYRUP CAKE
Rosanna Burr

Preparation 10 minutes   **Cook 10 minutes**

4 oz (113 grms) **plain flour**
2 medium **carrots chopped**
4 tbls **thin honey**
4 oz (113 grms) **butter**
½ teaspoon **vanilla essence**
½ teaspoon **bicarbonate of soda**
½ teaspoon **cinnamon**
½ teaspoon **ground nutmeg**
2 oz (56 grms) **walnuts chopped**

Syrup
2 tbls **orange juice**
2 tbls **thin honey**
2 oz (56 grms) **butter**

Topping
¼ **pint** (142 ml) **whipped cream**
2 oz (56 grms) **walnuts**
6½ **inch** (16 cm) **greased
and lined soufflé dish**

Place the eggs and carrots in a food processor and blend. Melt the butter in a large bowl on full power for 1–2 minutes. Add the honey and vanilla essence, then stir in the rest of the dry ingredients. Fold the egg and carrot mixture into the other mixture. Cook on low power for 7 minutes, and then on full power for 3 minutes. Leave to stand for 3 minutes and then turn the cake out and prick it well with a cocktail stick and pour the syrup over.

Syrup: Place the syrup ingredients in a pyrex jug and cook on full power for 1½ minutes until the mixture becomes a syrup, then pour the syrup over the cake and leave the cake until it is cold.

Topping: Decorate with the whipped cream and walnuts.

CRUNCHY JAM SQUARES
Jane Finestone

Preparation 5 minutes   **Cook 7½ minutes**   **Advance**   **Freezable**

6 oz (170 grms) **butter**
6 oz (170 grms) **soft dark brown sugar**
6 oz (170 grms) **porridge oats**
7 oz (200 grms) **plain flour**

½ teaspoon **salt**
½ teaspoon **baking powder**
4 oz (113 grms) **raspberry/plum jam**
8 **inch** (20 cm) **square baking dish greased**

Cream the butter and sugar in a large bowl until they are light and fluffy. Stir in the rest of the ingredients except the jam. Press half the mixture into the baking dish. Melt the jam on full power and pour onto the crumble mixture in an even layer. Spread the rest of the mixture over the jam and press it down lightly. Cook on full power for 7 minutes then leave it to stand for 5 minutes. Cut the crumble into squares and leave in the dish until cold. If freezing the crumble, freeze in the dish until required.

MARBLE CAKE
Anna Larking

Preparation 10 minutes   **Cook 11 minutes**   Advance   Freezable

Cake
6 oz (170 grms) **margarine/butter**
6 oz (170 grms) **caster sugar**
5 oz (142 grms) **self raising flour**
½ teaspoon **vanilla essence**
1 oz (28 grms) **cocoa sieved**
3 **eggs**
3 tbls **milk**
Few drops **red food colouring**

Filling
2 oz (56 grms) **butter**
3 oz (85 grms) **icing sugar sifted**
1 tbl **hot water**
1 dessertspoon **cocoa**

Topping
2 oz (56 grms) **melted chocolate**

Cake: Beat the butter and sugar together until fluffy, add the eggs and beat them, then mix in the flour. Beat in the milk. Divide the mixture into three bowls. Mix the cocoa into one bowl, a few drops of red colouring into another and the vanilla essence into the third bowl. Place alternate spoonfuls of the three varieties of mixture into a microwave cake dish which has been lined with greased, greaseproof paper. Smooth the top and cook on ¾ power for 7 minutes and then on full power for 4 minutes or, if preferred, on full power for 8 minutes. Turn the cake out and when cold cut it in half, horizontally. Spread one half with the filling and cover it with the other half.

Filling: Dissolve the cocoa in the water. Cream the butter and sugar and add to the cocoa.

Topping: Cover the top of the cake with the melted chocolate.

ORANGE CAKE
Jane Finestone

Preparation 5 minutes   **Cook 16 minutes**   Advance   **Freezable without icing**

8 fl oz (227 ml) **unsweetened orange juice**
9 oz (250 grms) **plain flour**
8 oz (225 grms) **granulated sugar**
2 **eggs separated**
4 oz (113 grms) **caster sugar**
3 teaspoons **baking powder**
½ teaspoon **salt**
8 fl oz (227 ml) **pure orange juice**
2 × 8 inch (20 cm) **round greased and floured baking dish**

Icing
2 oz (56 grms) **icing sugar**
2–3 tbls **orange juice**
Butter icing
2 oz (56 grms) **butter**
1 small **orange**
4 oz (113 grms) **icing sugar**

Whisk the egg whites until they form soft peaks. Beat in the caster sugar gradually until the mixture is thick and glossy. Place the flour, baking powder, salt, granulated sugar, oil and half the orange juice in another bowl and beat until light and fluffy. Fold in the egg white mixture. Divide the mixture between two cake dishes. Bake each one for 8 minutes on full power. Leave to stand in the dishes for 5 minutes covered with foil, then turn out and leave until cold on a wire rack.

To assemble: Sandwich the cake with orange butter icing and cover with orange glacé icing and a few crystallised orange slices.

Butter icing: Beat the butter until fluffy, then beat in the icing sugar and the grated rind of the orange with 2 teaspoons of the juice.

Glacé icing: Place the sifted icing sugar in a bowl and beat in the orange juice, if it is still very thick add enough cold water to make it into a smooth cream.

RASPBERRY MOUSSE CAKE   Caroline Young
Anchor Hocking MicroWare

6 oz (170 grms) **butter**	**1 tbl toasted flaked almonds**
6 oz (170) **caster sugar**	**1 lemon rind and juice**
3 eggs	**1 teaspoon baking powder**
6 oz (170 grms) **self raising flour**	**2 tbls icing sugar**
12 oz (340 grms) **raspberries**	**1½ teaspoons gelatine**
2 tbls orange flavoured liqueur	**1 egg white**
3 tbls orange juice	**5 fl oz** (142 ml) **double cream**
5 fl oz (142 ml) **thick natural yoghurt**	**MicroWare baking ring**

Cream the butter and sugar until light and fluffy. Gradually beat in the eggs, lemon peel and juice. Sift together the flour and baking powder, fold into the batter. Evenly spoon into the baking ring. Cook in a microwave oven on full power for approximately 7 minutes, or until outside is cooked – the top will still be moist. Let stand for 10 minutes, then turn out onto a cooling rack. When quite cold, slice a thin layer from the top of the cake. Set aside. Return rest of cake to washed baking ring. Using a grapefruit knife, cut out cake to leave a ½ inch (1 cm) thick shell. Purée 8 oz (225 grms) of raspberries, the icing sugar and liqueur in a liquidiser, sieve to remove the seeds. In a small bowl, sprinkle gelatine over the juice and cook in a microwave oven on full power for 30 seconds just to dissolve. Stir into purée. Beat egg white until stiff, lightly whip cream. Fold egg white and half the cream into the purée, together with reserved raspberries. spoon over top. Sprinkle with almonds. See page 67 for photograph.

To serve remove from dish onto a serving plate. Whisk yoghurt into reserved cream, spoon over top. Sprinkle with almonds. See page   for photograph.

RUM SAVARIN   Gillian Burr

Preparation 5 minutes	**Rising time 30 minutes**	**Cook 13 minutes**
		Freezable without syrup

8 oz (225 grms) **plain flour**	*Syrup*
½ teaspoon salt	**4 tbls brown rum**
2 teaspoons dried yeast	**4 tbls clear honey**
¼ pint (142 ml) + **3 tbls water**	**4 tbls apricot jam**
2 oz (56 grms) **butter**	**2 tbls water**
Few drops food colouring	
(optional)	*Garnish*
2 eggs beaten	**¼ pint** (142 ml) **double cream whipped**
8 inch (20 cm) **ring mould greased**	**Fresh fruit**

Place sugar and water in a jug and cook on full power for 30 seconds. Stir in the yeast and leave until frothy. Sift the flour with the salt and mix into the yeast mixture with a few drops of food colouring (optional), until the mixture becomes a soft dough. Cover with greased cling film and leave in a warm place until it doubles in size. Place butter in a bowl and cook on full power for 1 minute. Beat the eggs and butter into the yeast mixture and then pour the mixture into the mould. Cover again and leave until well risen. Cook on medium power for 10–12 minutes. Turn out.

Syrup: Place the syrup ingredients in a bowl, cover with pricked cling film and cook on full power for 3 minutes. Brush the syrup over the savarin. Cool, then decorate with the whipped cream piped round the edge of the plate and add some fresh fruit in the centre of the ring: strawberries, kiwi, cherries, or other preferred fruits.

INDEX

MEAT

POULTRY

VEGETABLES

SALADS

SAUCES, STUFFINGS AND PRESERVES

DESSERTS FOR MEAT MEALS

DESSERTS FOR MILK MEALS

SNACKS AND SUPPER DISHES

BISCUITS, BREADS, PETITS FOURS AND DRINKS